Entrepreneur® MAGAZINE'S

startup

Start Your Own

CAR WASH

Your Step-by-Step Guide to Success

Chris Simeral

EP
Entrepreneur
Press

Editorial Director: Jere L. Calmes
Managing Editor: Marla Markman
Cover Design: Beth Hansen-Winter
Production: Eliot House Productions
Composition: Tricia Miller

This publication is designed to provide accurate and authoritative information in regard to
the subject matter covered. It is sold with the understanding that the publisher is not
engaged in rendering legal, accounting or other professional services. If legal advice or other
expert assistance is required, the services of a competent professional person should be
sought.

Library of Congress Cataloging-in-Publication Data

Simeral, Chris.
    Start your own car wash/by Chris Simmeral.
       p.   cm.   —(Entrepreneur magazine's start up) (Entrepreneur Magazine's
business start-up series; guide #1076
    Includes index.
    ISBN 1-891984-91-8
    1. Car wash industry—Management. 2. New business enterprises—Management.
3. Entrepreneurship. I. Title: Car wash. II. Title. III. Series. IV. Entrepreneur
business start-up guide; no. 1076.

HD9999.C272S54 2003
629.28'7—dc21   2003044865

Printed in Canada

09 08 07 06 05 04   10 9 8 7 6 5 4 3 2

Contents

Preface ix

Chapter 1
Why Start a Car Wash Business? 1
  What a Car Wash Is and Isn't 2
    Myth #1: This Business Is a Cash Cow 3
    Myth #2: This Is a Hands-Off Business 3
    Myth #3: You Won't Have Employees
      to Worry About. 4
    Myth #4: You're in Total Control. 4
  Now for the Good News 4
  Past, Present, and Future 5
    Consolidation. 5
    The Changing Attitudes of Customers 5
    The Blurring of Your Core Business 6
    The Future. 7
  Your Entrepreneurial Spirit 7
  The Car Wash That's Right for You 9
  How Much Can You Really Make? 10

Chapter 2
Get to Know Your Market **13**
Who Is the Car Wash Customer? 14
Finding a Niche 15
    Fleet Washing 15
    Oversized Car Washes 15
What Customers Want. 16
    A Clean Car 16
    A Fair Price 16
    A Reasonable Amount of Time 18
    Value 18
Researching Your Market 19

Chapter 3
Location, Location, Location. **23**
Traffic Flow 24
Traffic Patterns. 25
Street Location. 26
Signage. 26
The Competition 26
Neighborhood Demographics 27
Local Government. 27
Weather 28
Proximity to Other Amenities 29
Labor Pool. 29

Chapter 4
Running Your Business **31**
A Day in the Life 32
    The Conveyor Car Wash Owner 32
    The Self-Serve Car Wash Owner. 33
What Are Your Goals? 36
Safety and Cleanliness 36

Chapter 5
Setting Up Shop. **39**
What Form Should Your Business Take? 40
The Experts 41
    Legal Eagles 41

Number-Crunchers 42
Insurance Agents 42
Repairpersons. 42
Architects 42
Insurance Issues 43
Should You Buy or Build Your Car Wash? 43
Should You Lease or Buy Your Land? 44
The Size of Your Lot 44
Lose Your Lease, Lose Your Wash 45
Always Push for Long Lease Terms 45
Options to Renew 45
What's a Good Lease Price? 46
Other Lease Factors. 47
Buying Your Land 47
Regulatory Issues 47
Testing the Waters 48
Environmental Studies 50
Naming Your Car Wash. 50
Writing Your Mission Statement 51

Chapter 6

Start-Up Expenses **53**

Where the Money Goes. 54
Office Equipment and Supplies 55
Computer System. 55
Computer Peripherals 55
Software 58
Phone System. 58
Miscellaneous Office Equipment 59
Office Furniture 60
Wash-Related Equipment 61
Establishing a Relationship with Your Distributor 61
New vs. Used Equipment. 62
Price vs. Reliability. 63
Self-Service Equipment 64
In-Bay Automatic Equipment. 67
Exterior-Conveyor and Full-Service Equipment 68
Retail/Lot Equipment 69
To Shade or Not to Shade 69

Security 70

Lighting 71

Signage. 72

Landscaping 72

Employees 73

Financing Your New Wash. 73

Chapter 7

Inventory and Pricing **79**

Basic Supplies for Your Car Wash 80

Simple Ways to Keep Track of Inventory. 81

Retail Items 81

Pricing Offline Items 82

Pricing Your Services 82

Pricing at a Self-Service Wash 83

Pricing at an In-Bay Automatic Wash 83

Pricing at a Conveyor Wash. 84

Your Menu of Services 84

Chapter 8

Car Wash Employees **87**

Service Writers/Greeters 88

Cashiers 90

Technicians. 91

Send-Off Employees 91

Where Can You Find Employees? 92

College Students 92

Retirees 93

Recent Immigrants. 93

Other Sources of Labor 94

How to Hire the Best Employees. 94

Overcoming the Dead-End Job Stigma 96

How Do You Retain Employees? 97

What Do You Want Your Incentive
    Program to Accomplish? 98

Offer Health Insurance and Benefits 99

Training Programs 99

Technical Training 99

Customer Service Training. 100

Turning Over Responsibilities 101
Knowing When to Let Them Go 102
Developing Your Employee Manual. 103

Chapter 9
Income and Expenses **107**
Evaluating Risk. 108
Your Rate of Return 108
Projecting Annual Revenue from an Existing Wash 109
Projecting Annual Revenue from a New Wash. 109
Operating Costs 113
For Example 113
Calculating Your Return on Investment 114
Revenue Streams 114
Vending Machines 115
Vacuum Services. 115
Gift Shops 116
Adding Offline Services 116
Other Automotive Services. 117
Should You Lease Your Extra Space? 118
Financial Management 118
Dealing with Taxes 119

Chapter 10
Advertising, Marketing, and Public Relations **123**
Coming Up with a Marketing Plan 124
Direct Mail. 124
Door-to-Door Marketing. 127
Database Marketing 128
Getting the Word Out 130
Exterior Signage. 130
Interior Signage 131
Product Sales and Placement 133
Media Advertising 133
Word-of-Mouth Advertising 134
Special Promotions. 134
Premium Deals. 134
One-Day-Only Specials 135
Frequent-Buyer Programs 136

Cross-Merchandising 137
Public Relations 137
    The Grand Opening. 137
    Charity Partnerships. 139
    Customer Relations 140
Measuring Your Success 140

Chapter 11
Long-Term Considerations **143**
    Expansion Into Other Services or Products 144
    Opening Satellite Locations 145
    Valuing and Selling Your Business 145
    What You Need to Succeed 146
        Location, Location, Location 147
        Service and Quality 147
        Price. 147
        Mechanical Skill 148
        Business Acumen 149
        Reliable Suppliers. 149
        Dedicated Employees. 150
        Repeat Customers 150
    Tales from the Trenches. 151
    The Bottom Line 154

Appendix
    Car Wash Resources. 155

Glossary **159**

Index **161**

Preface

When I first started researching the initial version of this book, we were right at the tail end of the dotcom boom. It seemed that everyone who was anyone was being turned into an instant millionaire (or even billionaire), fueled by the rampant speculation that the Internet would revolutionize the way the world did business. Well, we all know how that turned out. While technology has certainly changed most segments of the economy, and even completely transformed a few, the collapse of Internet mania proves that it's often the most basic ideas and businesses that last. Car washes are just such a business.

For as long as cars are around, their owners will need car washes. That's what makes car washes one of the more attractive start-ups out there. You can start as big or as small as you want, constrained only by the amount of start-up capital you can get your hands on and the time you're willing to spend to make the business a success. You can operate a small, self-serve operation in your spare time, or go all out with a complete full-service shop with a dozen employees or more. Either way, you'll undoubtedly face some challenges along the way, and that's what this guide is for.

You'll discover here what a car wash is, and, perhaps more importantly, what it isn't. Going into any business venture with your eyes open is vital to its eventual success—doubly so if you aren't just "trying it on for size," but instead intend on truly make a go of it. Keep your eyes open to the possibilities, and the drawbacks, with any site you examine for a new wash—and especially with the seller of an existing business who claims, whether honestly or not, to be "practically giving the thing away." Car washes are profitable businesses to be sure—but not all of them, no matter what the impression you get the next time you're stuck in line at your local wash is.

Finally, if there's one thing I discovered over the course of writing this book, it's that many people currently in the car wash business don't necessarily feel like talking about how they succeeded. The reason is simple—competition. No one wants a competing business right across the street, especially if that competitor is privvy to how you made your business work. But with that being said, there were some owners generous enough to share their time and expertise with me. I'd like to thank them for giving me many of the tips, tricks, and tactics for building a successful car wash business that you'll find in this book.

Why Start a Car Wash Business?

Y ou've probably never stopped to think about where your local car wash fits into the grand scheme of the car wash industry. The only thing you know is that when your car gets dirty you need to wash it, and the closest place to get that done is probably where you go.

Maybe you've spent some time considering opening a car wash business of your own while waiting in line for a wash on a bright and sunny Saturday morning. You've probably seen a dozen or more cars in queue, with each owner paying between $5 and $10 for a wash that they may not even be totally satisfied with. If you're like many entrepreneurs, you may have started doing some quick math in your head—projecting what the car wash owner is probably making in one month, then one year. Maybe you even thought "Boy, this place is a cash cow!"

Finally it's your turn. As you watch your car move through the tunnel, you see how automated the process is, how quickly it gets done, how little actual work seems to be required. "How hard could this possibly be? Anyone can make money running a car wash!" you might have thought.

Most car wash owners can share a wink and a smile at the naïveté of the average neophyte. Many people think a car wash is a great business opportunity because they see it as a business that doesn't require a great deal of hands-on work but still produces a great return on your investment. The reality is a bit more complicated than that. It's not exactly a mystery, but ask any car wash owner, and he will tell you the same thing—"It's not as easy as it looks."

What a Car Wash Is and Isn't

When most people think of a car wash, they tend to think of an exterior-conveyor wash. These are the washes that put cars on a motorized track and drag them through a tunnel where they are rinsed, soaped up, washed, rinsed again, and possibly waxed.

The cars then emerge clean (and perhaps even relatively dry) at the other end. But this is only one type of car wash. Other types of washes include the following:

Stat Fact
According to the president of the International Carwash Association, there are approximately 75,000 car washes in the United States.

- *Full-service.* This is basically a combination of the exterior conveyor with an additional inside cleaning.
- *In-bay automatic (also called a rollover).* This type of car wash is an automatic wash consisting of a machine that literally "rolls over" a stationary car parked in a washing bay.
- *Self-service.* Most self-service car washes are coin-operated brush-and-hose combinations that the driver uses to dispense soap, wash the car, and rinse it off.

We'll discuss in more detail what's involved with each of these types of washes in a minute. But for now, let's stick with the mental picture of the exterior-conveyor car wash as we learn more about the ins and outs of this business. The best place to start is by examining a few common misconceptions most people have about what a typical car wash business involves.

Myth #1: This Business Is a Cash Cow

Sure, if you drive by your local car wash on a sunny Saturday morning, you'll see cars waiting in line for a wash. But drive by that same car wash on a rainy Thursday afternoon, and you'll be lucky if you see one or two cars waiting. You might even see that the shop is closed for the day. Variables such as the time of the week, as well as the weather affect how profitable car wash businesses can be. And sometimes, people are content to let their cars stay dirty for "one more day."

Myth #2: This Is a Hands-Off Business

As an outsider, all you see are cars being dragged along a conveyor as a bunch of gizmos and doodads spray, buff, rinse, wax, and even dry them. You might not ever see a human being doing any work at all. In truth though, this is not a business that you can put on autopilot. For one thing, those gizmos and doodads can and will break down. And, depending on the type of equipment you buy, they might break down much more than you think.

Cars do emerge from those washing tunnels not clean enough to satisfy some customers or with a scratch that you didn't cause but that the customer blames you for anyway. Employees sometimes will not treat customers the way they should be treated, especially if you haven't trained them well. Shipments of supplies will be late, and someone (usually you) will have to be there to deal with it. After all, it's pretty much impossible to wash a car with no soap. The bottom line is that you'll be spending a lot of time at your car wash—at least until you learn the business well enough to be able to hire a professional manager who can take over when you're not there.

Myth #3: You Won't Have Employees to Worry About

This might actually be true for certain types of car washes (most likely self-service and, to a lesser extent, in-bay automatic washes), but for a full-service or exterior-conveyor wash, you're going to have to hire employees and inherit the headaches and responsibilities that go along with them. In fact, aside from the initial investment in equipment and commercial space, employees will probably be one of the biggest costs you incur while running your business.

Myth #4: You're in Total Control

Well, you are your own boss, that's for sure. But until someone figures out how to control factors such as the weather, you're still going to have to answer to a higher authority. No matter how much time you put into your business, there are still going to be things that go wrong—things you just can't control.

Even if you're a mechanical whiz, some of your equipment is going to break down. And if it happens at a peak washing time, like that glorious sunny Saturday morning we keep talking about, you're going to watch a lot of potential profit go down the drain.

You will have to suffer through days or maybe even weeks at a time (depending on where your business is located) when the weather is so bad that the farthest thing from anyone's mind is getting a car wash. And unfortunately, the bank won't care about the lousy weather when your loan payment comes due.

Now for the Good News

By now, you're probably having one of two reactions. You're either: a) sorry that you bought this book because what you've just learned is sapping your enthusiasm for opening a business that you thought would be a breeze, or, b) you're thankful that you bought this book because you think it may have saved you from wasting your money opening a business that you thought would be a breeze.

But before you start looking elsewhere for that great business opportunity, consider this: Many people have made a lot of money washing cars. It's a service that is always in demand and that most consumers are certainly willing to pay for.

The point in telling you about the pitfalls first is to make you think clearly and critically about just what it is you're getting into when you open a car wash. Yes,

there is the opportunity to make lots of money and have fun doing it—but only if you put in the work required to make your business a success. The rest of this book will deal with how to do just that. Let's get started by examining the origins of the industry, where it is right now, and where it might be headed in the near future.

Past, Present, and Future

"Just when I thought I understood the game, they changed the rules!" said Ben Alford of the International Carwash Association, in his state-of-the-industry address at the Car Care World Expo 2000.

Imagine sitting around a room and listening to a bunch of car wash vets waxing poetic about the good old days of the industry. If you eavesdropped on their conversation, you might hear them talking about the days when customers would come in for a full-service wash and think nothing of waiting an hour or more for the job to be completed. Or maybe they might talk about not having to compete with the latest dotcom start-up or fast-food chain for motivated employees. But whatever the specific topic of conversation, chances are it would center around one thing—how the industry has changed, and how they've had to adapt in order to build and grow their businesses.

Consolidation

One of the biggest changes occurring in the industry today is consolidation. Some companies apparently saw the same thing you did the last time you got your car washed, thought just as you did ("How hard could it be?"), and embarked on a car wash buying spree. One of the biggest consolidators is Mace, the same folks who make the pepper spray and the only one of the big consolidators that's a publicly traded company. So what happened to Mace when it started buying all these car washes? Its stock tumbled. According to Steve Gaudreau of Power Inc.'s Car Wash Institute, a training and consulting firm in Salem, Massachusetts, this was due in large part to the fact that the company simply underestimated the complexities of running a car wash. They found out the hard way just how hard it can be.

The Changing Attitudes of Customers

People today have less and less time to spend on errands such as getting their car washed. One of the main challenges of today's car wash owner isn't just providing customers with clean cars—it's providing customers with clean cars in as short a time as possible. Another challenge is providing the best quality of wash possible. Customers today are better educated about their options and demand more value for their money.

The Blurring of Your Core Business

It used to be that only oil companies offered a car wash with a fill-up. And then, more often than not, the wash would be free. Today, however, many car washes combine the services of a gas station and car wash, or they strike deals with neighboring filling stations for car wash discounts.

In the past, a customer would be lucky to get a free cup of coffee while waiting for his car to be washed. Today, the average car wash customer is likely to find a wide array of snack foods at his disposal in the car wash "gift shop." Some owners even sell greeting cards and pocketbooks alongside the more traditional air fresheners and key chains in their gift shop.

What this points to is a trend toward offering customers multiple services all in one place—a one-stop shopping experience. This only makes sense, since the average customer is more pressed for time than ever before. The more you can combine the services they need, the more likely customers will be to pick your car wash over another.

According to a recent survey published in *Auto Laundry News*, almost half (46 percent) of car wash owners say that having a gas station nearby that offers a free wash

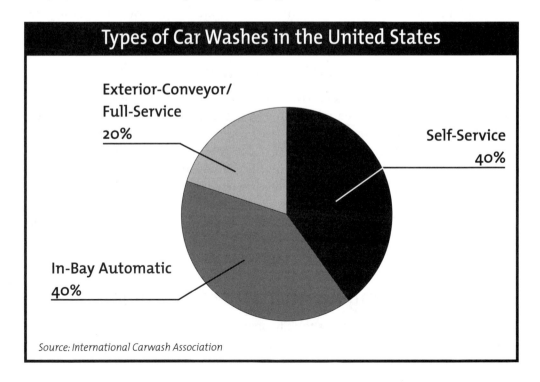

Types of Car Washes in the United States

Exterior-Conveyor/
Full-Service
20%

Self-Service
40%

In-Bay Automatic
40%

Source: International Carwash Association

Stat Fact
According to Dick H., a car wash owner in Sacramento, California, if you take longer than 18 minutes to wash someone's car, chances are you won't see them again. Not only do you have to provide a great wash, but you're also going to have to do it quicker than ever before in order to succeed.

with a gas purchase has hurt their business. While that's significant, the fact that the free wash doesn't take even more business away may be due to the fact that washing cars is a side business for these gas stations, and they tend not to do as good a job as a dedicated car wash. So while you may choose to offer multiple services to your customers to enhance your business, don't forget that your primary business is offering a quality car wash.

The Future

Let's face it, if the experts 50 years ago were right, we'd all be flying around in rocket cars by now. While no one can predict the future with accuracy, what we can say is that current trends certainly favor car wash owners. People are buying more-expensive vehicles, and they're keeping them longer and want to maintain them in good condition. And while we may see some dramatic design changes in cars over the coming years—it may soon be the case that we "charge" our cars at home rather than filling them up at the gas station—the business of the car wash owner doesn't seem at risk. No matter what happens, it is likely that as long as there are cars, there will always be a need for car washes.

With that said, you're about to enter an industry that is in flux. Some say that the time has never been better for newcomers. Others caution that until the industry "shakes out," committing the time and money required to make a new car wash successful is a risky proposition. Every entrepreneurial endeavor involves risk, and you will have to research your local market diligently and assess your chances for success.

Your Entrepreneurial Spirit

You will also need to evaluate whether a car wash is the right type of business for you. Will you enjoy the tasks that come along with it—fixing machinery, keeping supplies on hand, meeting and dealing with customers, resolving conflicts and crises? Take the self-quiz on page 8 to find out how well-suited you are to working in the car wash industry.

For starters, how energetic are you? If you're someone who falls asleep in front of the TV every night at eight o'clock, you may not be able to put in the time and energy

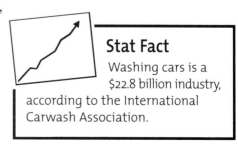

Stat Fact
Washing cars is a $22.8 billion industry, according to the International Carwash Association.

needed to make your business a success. If, on the other hand, you're a dynamo—someone who enjoys expending energy and isn't happy unless you're on the go—you'll have a better chance of being an entrepreneurial success.

How risk-tolerant are you? Starting any business involves a certain amount of risk-tolerance. You won't be getting a steady paycheck anymore, and it's likely that your income will vary widely from week to week and month to month. This isn't only true when you're starting a business—it will probably continue for months or even years. You're going to have your slow months, and you're going to have your hot months. How well can you weather the ebb and flow? If you can absorb the hits you're going to take when money is slow to come in, you're going to be able to stick around and

Personality Traits and Preferences Self-Quiz

Are you the type of person who should own a car wash? All of the personality traits or preferences listed below would be helpful to a new car wash owner. While there's no score that either qualifies or disqualifies you for car wash ownership, if you check the "false" column frequently, you may want to reconsider whether you would enjoy this line of work.

Traits or Preferences	True	False
I like working with my hands.	❏	❏
I like meeting new people.	❏	❏
I have a tolerance for financial risk.	❏	❏
I enjoy learning about how mechanical things work.	❏	❏
I have a basic knowledge of business and can learn to keep accurate financial records.	❏	❏
I don't mind a fluctuating income from month to month.	❏	❏
Long hours at work don't bother me.	❏	❏
If something breaks around the house, I can usually figure out how to fix it.	❏	❏
Manual labor isn't a problem for me.	❏	❏
I can work on my own, without a boss to provide direction.	❏	❏

enjoy it when business picks up again. In short, you shouldn't be someone who wants to throw in the towel at the first sign of trouble.

How self-motivated are you? Are you someone who stops trying to improve something when you feel that it's "good enough"? To be sure, there's something to be said for leaving well enough alone. But unless you're constantly striving to take steps to make your business even better, you run the risk of having your business become stale. No one would want the economy as a whole to just remain where it is right now and not grow, and it's the same thing with your car wash. If you make $100,000 in your first year, are you the kind of person who's going to push yourself to make $125,000 the next? Do you need someone to give you the motivation to do that, or can you find the motivation within yourself? After all, if you aren't concerned about growing your business, who will be?

The Car Wash That's Right for You

As mentioned earlier, there are really four distinct types of car washes that you might choose to operate. Gaudreau, of Power Inc.'s Car Wash Institute, says that trying to offer general advice on starting and successfully running a car wash business is a bit like trying to tell someone how to start and run a successful restaurant. You can't really answer the question until you decide what type of restaurant (or, in this case, car wash) you want.

If you haven't done so already, now is the time to think about what type of car wash you want to own. Some of the factors to consider in making your decision include

- the amount of capital you have at your disposal,
- the amount of time you want to spend running the business, and
- the amount of money you're hoping to make.

In general, the type of car wash that's going to require the biggest investment from you, both in terms of time and money, is a full-service wash. That's also the type that tends to generate the most revenue. But unless you have $1 million or more to invest up front, it's probably not the best choice. Moving down the line, an exterior-conveyor car wash is the next highest in terms of start-up costs, followed by an in-bay automatic car wash, and finally, a self-service car wash.

Each type of car wash has its advantages in terms of time and capital investment vs. profit potential. If your goal is simply to make extra money to supplement another income, consider sticking to a car wash with a few self-service bays—at least initially. If this new business is intended to be your life's pursuit

Fun Fact

The world's first car wash opened in 1914 in Detroit. It was called "The Automated Laundry."

Which Car Wash Is Right for You?

Type of Wash	Start-Up Costs	Time Needed	Profit Potential	Required Knowledge
Full-service	High	Intensive	High	Mechanical and general business knowledge a must
Exterior-conveyor	High (somewhat lower labor costs than full-service)	Intensive (slightly lower than full-service)	High	Mechanical and general business knowledge
In-bay automatic	Medium	Medium (significantly less than a full-service or exterior-conveyor car wash)	Medium	Mechanical, some basic knowledge of business practices
Self-service	Low to medium	Low to medium	Low to medium	Mechanical, some basic knowledge of business practices

and your primary income, you're probably going to need a full-service or exterior-conveyor car wash to make that happen. Another factor affecting how much start-up capital you'll need is whether you want to lease or buy an existing business, or start fresh by building a brand-new facility of your own. Take a look at the chart above to compare some of the tradeoffs involved in selecting what type of car wash to open.

How Much Can You Really Make?

You wouldn't be getting into this business if you didn't think there was the opportunity to turn a healthy profit. But how much can you really expect to make? Because we're not discussing a one-size-fits-all business when we talk about a car wash, how much you can make is dependent on a number of factors. Ask yourself the following questions to get a handle on what you can expect:

- *What type of car wash will you operate (exterior-conveyor, full-service, in-bay automatic, or self-service)?* In general, the more services you provide, the more money you're going to make. A full-service car wash, which frequently "up-sells" customers, has a higher profit potential than a self-service car wash.
- *How much business will your location support?* If your full-service car wash is in an area filled with high-income professionals driving European sports cars, it's

probably going to do better than if it's located in a low-income neighborhood or an economically depressed town. Different areas will demand different types of car washes. While an affluent neighborhood may have a greater market for full-service car washes, a moderate- to low-income area might have greater market demand for in-bay automatic or self-service car washes. In short, you must match your services

Stat Fact

According to a recent survey by *Auto Laundry News,* the car wash industry is growing. More than half of car wash operators said that they washed more cars in the year surveyed than in the previous year.

with the demands of the neighborhood in which you'll do business.

Beyond these basics, there are the factors that determine the success of any business—how successful you are at marketing and selling your services, keeping costs under control, hiring quality employees, and so on. With that said, here are some general guidelines for the profit potential of the four types of car washes we've mentioned:

1. *Full-service car wash:* $400,000 to $750,000 a year

2. *Exterior-conveyor car wash:* $100,000 to $375,000 a year

3. *In-bay automatic car wash (a "3 and 1" combination of self-service and in-bay automatic wash bays, discussed in Chapter 4):* $50,000 to $100,000 a year

4. *Self-service car wash (assuming a four-bay, self-service facility):* $40,000 to $80,000 a year

Now that you know the basics of the car wash industry, it's time to move on to the nitty-gritty of running and building your business. In Chapter 2, we'll delve into the foundation of starting your car wash business—carefully researching your market.

Get to Know
Your Market

It's tempting to say that anyone who owns a car, truck, bus, or other motorized vehicle is a potential customer of your car wash. In a sense, that's true. But it's not exactly specific enough to allow you to develop an accurate business plan. Consultants who help car wash entrepreneurs open new businesses ask dozens of questions before passing judgment on the viability of a new site, and they charge a hefty fee for the service. To truly give your-self the best opportunity to succeed, you'll need to ask some of those same questions. Let's start by defining exactly who your customers will be.

Who Is the Car Wash Customer?

There are several types of car wash customers. Some you can serve no matter what type of car wash you have, while others will require a car wash with specialized equipment if you hope to capture their business. For example, if you want to wash large trucks, you're going to need special equipment designed for this purpose (see the "Oversized Car Washes" section on page 15 for more information).

Here are the various market segments of potential customers and some general information about each:

- *Home washers.* Home washers account for about 50 percent of the total public, according to the International Carwash Association (ICA). As you might expect, home washers tend to live in suburban communities and have average incomes. It's also likely that these washers live in single-family homes, where they have space to wash their cars on their own. It's very unlikely, for instance, that people who live in high-rise buildings in the city will have the space necessary to wash cars on their own.

    Although the costs associated with hand washing a car at home, both in terms of supplies and time, may make it less economical than getting a bare-bones package at a professional car wash, these "noncustomers" still see doing it themselves as a money-saving proposition. If you can find a way to capture this market, either through promotions or by appealing to their sense of environmental concerns (most of the public is unaware that professional washes are actually better for the environment that hand-washing at home), you can effectively double your customer base.

- *Self-service washers.* The self-service car wash patron is typically a renter. Since they don't own a home and may have little space to wash a car where they live, a professional facility is a necessity. They're also a bit more cost-conscious than those who frequent full-service or exterior-conveyor washes, and tend to have slightly lower incomes. Men tend to use self-serves more than women, according to research by ICA.

> **Stat Fact**
> According to a recent survey by *Professional Carwashing & Detailing* magazine, the majority of self-service car washes (41.2 percent) are located in suburban areas. Urban areas come in second, with just over 31 percent.

- *In-bay automatic, exterior-conveyor, and full-service washers.* Research by ICA suggests that women are more likely to use the services of an automatic wash, perhaps because of the convenience. As you might expect, the typical patron of an automatic wash is a bit more affluent than the self-service customer, choosing to pay to have their car washed away from home, even though most are homeowners with space to do it themselves. The most affluent of all car wash customers are those who patronize full-service washes, just as you might expect.

The ICA goes to great expense to compile statistical data on car wash customers' attitudes and preferences, and these reports are available to ICA members only. The ICA is an organization that you'll probably want to join as soon as possible to gain access to the wealth of information they've accumulated that can help you grow your business.

Finding a Niche

For the most part, you can expect the bulk of your business to come from the traditional source—individual car owners. But there are other market segments that can be profitable as well. Here are a few ideas for how you might be able to serve a special market and fill a niche within the industry.

Fleet Washing

Think about how many types of businesses or government agencies there are that you might be able to target. Police departments, auto repair shops, auto rental agencies, and new or used car dealers are just a few of the different organizations that need to wash many cars on a regular basis. If you're creative, you should be able to come up with ways to service these markets, no matter what type of car wash you have.

An agreement to service a fleet of police cruisers, for example, might take one of several forms. You could charge a flat monthly fee and agree to provide a certain number of washes during the month. Alternatively, and this is more suited to a self-service or in-bay automatic car wash, you might provide car wash tokens at a discounted price. For a full-service or exterior-conveyor car wash, you could simply log the number of times a police cruiser uses the wash, and then bill the department each month on a discounted scale. Just about any type of arrangement is possible. The only drawback is that because you're providing discounts, your margins will be smaller. But most car wash owners say the volume more than makes up for it.

Oversized Car Washes

How many times have you been behind a filthy semi and seen the words "Wash Me" carved out of the dirt and grime. There's a reason for this: Most traditional car washes simply aren't equipped to handle the "big rigs," and you can take advantage of that fact. If you're dead set on opening a car wash but can't find a suitable location, you might want to look into opening a specialty wash that caters to oversized vehicles. Your business model here will be somewhat different from the standard car wash that serves the general consumer, but the basics of how you'll succeed are still the same. You'll need to be located where these oversized vehicles travel and preferably stop—perhaps at a rest area along a well-traveled truck route, such as I-95 in the eastern United States.

If you're planning to open this type of car wash, it's very important to make sure any prospective site is able to accommodate the large washing machinery that's required. The easiest and best way to do this is to consult manufacturers of this equipment to find out exactly what you'll need in terms of space.

What Customers Want

No surprise here: a clean car at a fair price in a reasonable amount of time. But what that means might vary depending on the customer. For example, a car owner who has become accustomed to full-service treatment would probably find the process of washing his car at a self-service wash unacceptable. Similarly, a customer used to the relatively quick process involved in an in-bay automatic wash probably won't be happy waiting 15 or 20 minutes for a full-service wash. What this demonstrates is that "a clean car at a fair price in a reasonable amount of time" doesn't necessarily mean the same thing to every customer.

A Clean Car

How you define a clean car and how your customers define a clean car may be different. For some car wash owners, a clean car means whatever the end result is of one trip through the tunnel. For others, especially full-service car wash owners, a clean car means one that is spotless inside and out. Although today's automatic equipment is pretty good, it's probably going to require at least some form of hand washing to get a spotless car. For a self-service washer, a clean car is going to be whatever the owner decides is clean.

You're going to have to decide what degree of clean you'll be aiming for at your car wash. There will be some customers who are never satisfied, while others will be happy as long as your equipment does a decent job. It's how you handle the hard-to-please variety that will define your service.

A Fair Price

In general, the price you charge is going to have to be about the same price others in your area are charging. There's very little you can do to change that. With that said,

What's Important When Choosing a Wash?

Customers who typically wash their cars at home can be persuaded to let professionals do it instead—but first you'll have to convince them that there's a reason to switch. By knowing the factors that would be most likely to bring a home washer to your shop, you can tailor your services, approach, or price accordingly.

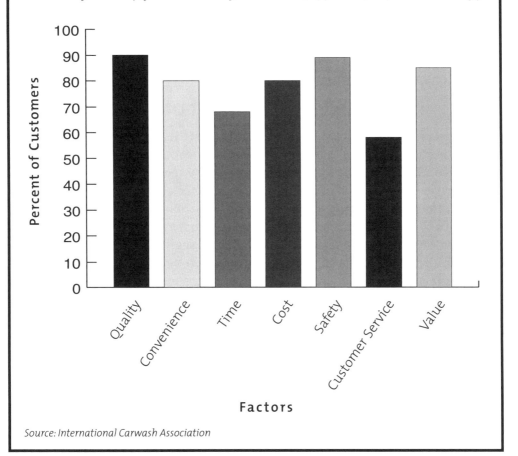

Source: International Carwash Association

you don't have to compete with every car wash in your neighborhood. You'd never think about charging the low prices of an in-bay automatic for a complete full-service wash, for example. Similarly, you may be able to get away with charging a bit more if you offer extra amenities or a far superior wash. But most of the time you and your competitors will wind up charging just about the same price, with one undercutting the other slightly—depending on the level of competition.

If you are able to offer a superior level of service, or some other attraction that makes your wash much more desirable than any other, a customer's perception of a

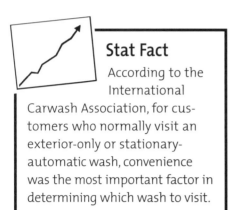

Stat Fact

According to the International Carwash Association, for customers who normally visit an exterior-only or stationary-automatic wash, convenience was the most important factor in determining which wash to visit.

fair price may change—but probably only slightly. It's also a bit risky to assume that if you build a better mousetrap, the world will beat a path to your door. Getting a car wash isn't like buying another product or service that is highly differentiated. For better or worse, most people think that they're going to get just about the same level of service, no matter where they go. In other words, most of your customers will think "A car wash is a car wash."

A Reasonable Amount of Time

Remember back in Chapter 1 when we mentioned the full-service car wash owner who has seen the patience of his customers decline steadily over the years? When he first got into the business, it was common for his customers to think nothing at all at waiting 45 minutes or more for a full-service wash to be completed. Today, that same owner says anything more than 18 minutes and he's going to lose business. That's a trend that's continuing just about everywhere. Customers want the same thing they got before, only better and faster. Estimating how long your customers will view as reasonable depends on what they've come to expect from other washes in your area. If 30 minutes is the average, then you should expect to match that or risk losing customers. If you can beat the average time, it could become one of the major selling points of your business.

For a self-service wash, this concept is turned on its head. People are paying for time in a self-service wash, and they want as much of it as they can get. To compete as a self-service, you're probably going to have to offer at least as much time for each token (dollar, quarter, or whatever) as your competitors.

Value

Here are some things to consider when you ask if you're providing what the typical car wash customer is looking for:

- *How do your prices compare to the competition?* If your competitors are all offering their services for a substantially cheaper price, you're going to have a hard time satisfying customers, even if you manage to attract them in the first

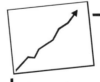

Stat Fact

According to the International Carwash Association, customers who typically use a full-service wash say the quality of service is the single most important factor that determines which car wash they use.

place. In other words, a fair price is relative to what your competitors in your area charge.

- *How does your service compare?* Are your competitors' employees dressed in uniforms while yours are in tattered jeans? Do you have a skilled service writer and staff who know how to satisfy customers' needs? Does your competition? Remember, car wash customers may be willing to pay a bit more for friendly service.

- *How does your wash compare?* The bottom line is that, no matter how low your price, if you aren't cleaning cars properly, people are not going to use your car wash. That's one reason car wash owners aren't terribly worried about cheap or even free washes that some gas stations provide. Since washing cars is not their core business, gas stations usually won't provide the level of service and attention to detail that a car wash provides.

- *Can you offer one-stop shopping?* Another approach to consider is offering your customers as many amenities as possible to make it easier for them to get as many errands done in one place as they can. For example, many car wash customers prefer to combine a trip to the gas station with a car wash. This may or may not be feasible for you, depending on the volume of business you'll do. Oil companies may be reluctant to make deliveries to your station if you aren't moving enough of their product. It might be a better idea to explore cross-marketing opportunities with a station nearby. It's not exactly one-stop shopping, but it's close.

Researching Your Market

Here are some of the things you'll want to find out about the market in your area.

- *Your potential customers.* You may be able to acquire information about your target market from the U.S. Census Bureau or your local municipality's planning department. The types of things you'll want to know about your potential customers include: average income, what percentage rent and what percentage own their homes, how many cars the typical family owns, and whether the typical family leases or owns their car.

- *Your competition.* You'll need to know what kind of competition you'll be up against. Try finding out these things about other area washes:
  - *Average cost for a basic exterior wash*
  - *Average cost for the most expensive package*
  - *Average cost of one minute of time (for self-service owners only)*
  - *Average time for completion of basic (or full-service) wash cycle*

– *Number of self-service bays within three miles of your location (for self-service owners only)*

– *Number of full-service washes within three miles of your location (for full-service owners)*

– *Extra services (waxing, vacuuming, etc.) offered most often*

– *Most common products dispensed from vending machines*

– *Average age of existing facilities (important if you decide to modernize an existing car wash)*

Stat Fact
More than 65 percent of automatic wash owners own only a single location, according to *Professional Carwashing & Detailing* magazine.

We've provided a "Market Research Checklist" on page 21 for you to use while gathering information on the market in your area. You will also want to refer to this checklist as you read through the next chapter, which deals with researching and choosing a location for your business.

Market Research Checklist

Here is some of the information you'll need to know about your market.

Information to Gather	Check When Done
Population within two miles of car wash site?	
Population within three miles of car wash site?	
Population within five miles of car wash site?	
Traffic flow: How many cars pass by your proposed site on an average day?	
Traffic patterns: What is the speed limit on the adjacent road?	
Housing: Comprised mainly of single-family homes or apartment buildings?	
Street location: Corner or midblock?	
Competition: Number of car washes within three miles of your site?	
Amenities: Number of convenience stores or other businesses in the immediate area?	
Labor pool: Is there an adequate source of labor in your neighborhood?	
Average household income within three miles of your site?	

3

Location, Location, Location

Whether you're talking about office space, a hotel, a supermarket, or a car wash, location is one of the most important factors (if not the most important) in creating a successful business. "I've known a lot of bad car washes in good locations that have done very well," says one car wash

Stat Fact
According to
Dultmeier Sales,
a car wash equipment manufacturer based in Omaha,
Nebraska, the ideal traffic
speed on the road adjacent
to your car wash is 40 mph.

consultant we interviewed. "And I've known a lot of great car washes that have been in poor locations that didn't do well."

In the car wash business, a good location can mean many different things. First of all, the location has to be a good match for the type of car wash you're operating. For example, a full-service car wash will generally be a better fit for an affluent community, where there are lots of owners of expensive cars who are willing to spend a little more money to keep them clean. A self-service wash might be a better fit for a community where car owners are more cost-conscious. Here are some other rules of thumb you should follow when evaluating a prospective site.

Traffic Flow

There's an old saying about a successful salesman that says, "He could sell ice to an Eskimo." You may be that type of person. You may be the greatest salesman in the world, but if you're trying to sell car wash services in an area where there are no cars, you're going to have a problem. Generally, the most successful washes are located on busy (but not incredibly fast-moving) thoroughfares.

Before you even think about designing your car wash, you'll want to scout several possible locations and measure the traffic flow. How many cars pass by each hour? When is the traffic heaviest? If you're doing the study yourself, you may want to actually stand on the site and watch the cars drive by to see what types of cars the people are driving. Do this a few times and you'll begin to get an idea for what type of wash the area might support. You can also contact government agencies such as the U.S. Census Bureau to obtain true demographic data, which will aid you in determining what type of wash might work best in a particular area. If you're buying an existing wash, this data will probably be available from the previous owner. If you're planning to build one, you'll have to come up with this information on your own.

Stat Fact
Fifty-nine percent
of self-service
owners report having a traffic
light within one block of the
entrance to their location,
according to a recent survey by
*Professional Carwashing &
Detailing* magazine.

Local government agencies may also be another source for information on traffic flow. For example, you might try contacting your city or state's planning or roads department to see if it has traffic-flow data. The department should be able to provide you with information that will give you a good idea of how many cars generally pass by your site on any given day. Do whatever you have to to get an accurate estimate of this—it's one of the most important things you can know about the viability of a car wash business.

Traffic Patterns

Perhaps just as important as the number of cars that pass by your location is how the cars pass by. As mentioned above, a busy street isn't enough. You also want to look at the speed of the cars. Think about your own driving patterns. You're probably much more likely to pull off the road to visit a merchant when you don't have to slam on the brakes to do it. Similarly, fast-moving traffic leaves very little time for you to spot stores on the side of the road if you don't know exactly what you're looking for. If the traffic is moving too fast, you'll have less chance of capturing customers who just happen to drive by and spot your car wash.

Capture Caper

Your capture rate—the percentage of cars that drive by your wash and actually stop to patronize your business—is one of the most important statistics for any car wash owner. There are many factors that will affect your capture rate, including the speed limit, the presence of traffic lights or stop signs, your visibility from the road, the ease of entrance and exit from your lot, and the presence of other businesses that help to keep drivers alert to what's available along the side of the road.

Once you know the average traffic flow each day you can expect, then you need to turn your attention to determining the capture rate you can expect. This information will help you get a solid idea of just how many customers you can expect every day. If you're buying an existing car wash, the current owner should be able to provide this information. A recent survey by *Professional Carwashing & Detailing* magazine found that capture rates ranged from 0.45 percent for exterior-only conveyor washes to 0.52 percent for full-service washes. That was significantly lower than numbers reported the previous year (0.76 percent for exterior-only and 0.56 percent for full-service).

To use your capture rate to compute an average number of customers a day, multiply the traffic count by your anticipated capture rate. For example:

20,000 cars a day x .0045 *(representing a 0.45 percent capture rate)* =
90 customers a day

Stat Fact

Most surveys, like those conducted by the International Carwash Association and *Auto Laundry News*, find that around 90 percent of customers generally travel ten miles or fewer to get to a car wash.

Street Location

Ideally, you'd like to be located on a busy corner with a stoplight, on a heavily traveled road. The traffic light forces cars to stop and gives drivers ample opportunity to pull into your wash. You also want to have easy access to your car wash, preferably with a driveway right off the road. This should be something you're able to determine simply by driving the road yourself. If you can answer "yes" to the question, "Is this location easy and convenient for cars on this road to see and get to?" then it's probably a good location.

Signage

You'll have to consider what you'll actually be able to construct by way of signage in your prospective location. You should first check with the local government to determine what you'll legally be allowed to construct. Large signs that dominate the landscape might not be permitted in some areas. In other areas, this may not be a problem as long as you meet certain requirements. The only way to find out is to check on the regulations beforehand.

Assuming that the laws aren't too restrictive, the next step is to determine what kind of signage the site can support and where it will be visible to drivers on the road. You'll want to have enough space to construct your sign in an area that maximizes its visibility to drivers. If you're behind a building, around a sharp bend in the road, or some other less-than-ideal situation, you might find that no matter what kind of sign you construct, it's going to be nearly impossible for your potential customers to spot. Try walking along the road, rather than driving it, so you can see in more detail exactly where the blind spots might be. All other things being equal, the better site is the one that gives your car wash maximum exposure.

The Competition

Is there another car wash right across the street from the site you're considering? Is there one down the road? Is there one at the corner a short distance away, while your site is in the middle of a block? These are obvious factors you'll want to consider when evaluating a site. But there are other, more subtle ones, as well.

Stat Fact

According to a recent survey from *Auto Laundry News*, more than 50 percent of car wash owners reported having more than two competitors in their area.

For example, is there a gas station nearby? Even if they don't offer car washes yet, they certainly may in the future. Is there a lube shop or car repair center? Again, more potential competitors. We're not saying that the mere presence of competition will kill your car wash. Maybe, with a combination of better service and better prices, you could win the battle for customers. But if it's a choice between two otherwise promising sites—one with no competition and one with plenty of competition—it should be an easy choice.

> ### Smart Tip
> Tip...
>
> Don't give up on a location just because it's in a low-income area. For just about any community, there's a type of wash that's right.

While it is generally true that the less competition you have, the better off you are, don't panic and dismiss a site out of hand simply because of the perceived threat of competition. Remember what we've been saying all along: There are really three types of car washers—those who wash their cars at home, those who prefer to wash their own cars but lack the facilities (i.e., your typical self-service customer), and those who want their cars washed for them. It's rare that these customer groups will cross over in any extensive way, so it depends on what type of car wash opens near you.

Neighborhood Demographics

Different types of washes can, and do, succeed in different types of communities. Whether or not the community you're considering is right for the type of car wash you want to open is a matter of some background research. Start by determining what type of wash you'll be able to operate given the space you have available. It may be that you simply don't have enough room for the kind of car wash that fits the community.

You'll also want to look at the type of housing that exists in the area surrounding your prospective site. Generally, apartment complexes are better than single-family housing. This is true for a couple of reasons. First, lots of apartment buildings mean you have a higher population density in the area. Second, apartment-dwellers generally don't have a driveway or access to an outside water source to wash their cars. This segment of the market is usually obligated to visit a professional car wash—or else let their cars stay dirty.

Local Government

The local zoning laws of the community, and the support you can expect to receive from the local government and residents, are crucial factors in your site-selection process. In many cases, car washes are still suffering from the public perception that they are somehow "seedy" businesses that employ drifters and bring an unwanted element into a community. Although this really isn't the case, old attitudes and prejudices die hard.

Many owners have had to put up with years of haggling and legal battles just to win the right to open a new car wash. Oftentimes they simply give up, figuring that the fight isn't worth whatever they might potentially gain from owning the business. This may be what some local government officials are banking on—if they make it hard enough, word will get out that it's more trouble than it's worth to open a car wash in their area.

You will need to investigate the regulations governing any prospective site you have under consideration. Say, for example, that you've found a prime location just off a busy roadway. Local zoning regulations may require that you need an inordinate amount of space to account for waiting lines, which could scuttle your initial plans for the size of your site and how much of it can be used for actual wash bays. Another potential problem involves roadway expansion. It has happened that potential owners have seen their lot size effectively and dramatically decreased because the local government wanted to keep the option of widening the road at some unspecified date in the future. The lesson? Before you invest your time and money in a new site, make sure the powers that be won't throw you a curve ball.

There's yet another way the government can scuttle your car wash plans before they get started, and this involves impact fees. The way they see it, your car wash is going to affect the surrounding environment. And by environment, we don't mean the air and water. Instead, what they're most likely going to be talking about is the roadway. Depending on where you choose to set up shop, you could be hit with a penalty of sorts that will result from the number of cars the local government expects to come to you for a wash. The theory is that were your wash not there, those cars wouldn't travel the roadway and wouldn't contribute to the wear and tear on the asphalt. In essence, because of you, the road is going to deteriorate just a bit faster than it would have if people stayed home to wash their cars. Whether or not this is true really doesn't matter. If they say it's so, then it's so, and you'd better plan on getting out your checkbook.

Weather

This variable will have more to do with the area of the country in which you locate your car wash rather than the area of town where you put down stakes. People don't wash their cars when it's raining—that much is clear. So if you plan on opening your wash in a rainy climate, you may have more days of slow business than if you settled in a drier climate.

This doesn't mean car washes can't be successful all over the country. There are plenty of successful car wash businesses in Seattle, just as there are plenty of successful car wash businesses in Los Angeles, but it is a factor to keep in mind.

Not surprisingly, surveys show that the best time of year for most car washes is in the winter. Road salt, snow, slush, and the other side effects of inclement weather that occur in the northern half of the country make this a boom time for many businesses.

But if you live in warmer, sunnier climates, you may benefit from the fact that there are fewer rainy days to cut into your business. In the end, it might be a trade-off, but the weather is a factor to consider when you develop your business plan.

Proximity to Other Amenities

The majority of today's car wash customers want to make their lives easier by combining a trip to the car wash with other errands. In surveys, more customers say they would rather combine the act of getting a car wash with getting a tank of gas than any other errand. If you happen to be located near or even right next to a busy gas station, you in essence have a partner working for you to pull customers in to your location. Some car wash owners have worked out arrangements with gas stations to give reduced-price washes with any fill-up or when a certain amount of gas is purchased. This kind of arrangement helps you and the station. It encourages customers to fill their tanks or buy more gas than they might normally and drives these same customers (who otherwise might have gone elsewhere or simply gone without) into your car wash.

Another business that can help attract customers to your car wash is a convenience store. Again, many washes located adjacent to convenience stores are able to work out an arrangement in which the store gives discount coupons for washes to its customers. If you wind up paying for the entire discount it may decrease your "per car sales," but especially on a slow day, it can keep a steady flow of cars coming through your wash.

It's not uncommon for this relationship to go the other way, too. It's not unheard of, and is in fact fairly common, for owners of convenience stores to install some sort of car wash facilities on their premises—assuming, of course, that they have the space for such an expansion. The reason for this is that the business flows both ways. Car wash facilities attract convenience store customers and convenience stores attract car wash customers. We'll discuss how to capitalize on a relationship with a convenience store in a later chapter. But for now, just take it on faith that it's a plus if one is nearby, and even a bigger plus if there's one right next door.

Labor Pool

Unless you're operating only the smallest of self-service washes, you're probably going to need to hire employees. This means you're going to need an available pool of qualified job candidates. We'll get into more detail about what to look for in employees in Chapter 8, but for now it's important to think about what kind of worker you'll have available in your particular area. If you suspect there will be a shortage of people willing to work at a car wash in your area, recognize that you're probably going to have to pay more for labor and that you may have a harder time finding workers no matter how much you're willing to pay.

It's a plus if you're located in an area where the traditional sources of car wash labor are also located—for example, if there's a college or high school nearby. If you see many fast-food restaurants or convenience stores in your area, two other businesses that typically employ unskilled workers, that's a pretty good indication that potential employees are around. Though it can also mean you'll have to compete with these other businesses for good workers.

Now that we've discussed what to look for when you're scouting potential locations, let's turn to how you'll run the business you're going to build. In Chapter 4, you'll learn about the general tasks involved in running a car wash business.

Running
Your Business

Most car wash owners say there really isn't a typical day that can be applied across the board to all owners. How you run your business day to day will depend on some of the key decisions you make when you're starting up. For example, will this business be your sole source of income? Will you be operating a full-service car wash or a self-service car wash? If you decide on a self-service car wash, how many bays will you have? Will they all be in one location, or will they be spread around town? These are all factors that will eventually determine what your day will be like as a car wash owner.

A Day in the Life

Up to this point, we've been discussing the four distinct types of car washes. In this chapter, we'll combine them into just two categories—conveyor (which includes exterior-only and full-service washes) and self-serve (which includes true self-service wand bays and in-bay automatic roll-over units)—because many of the responsibilities overlap. For example, the owner of a conveyor wash that provides exterior cleaning only is going to have a similar typical day to the owner of a conveyor wash that includes interior cleaning services, too.

The Conveyor Car Wash Owner

Assuming that you're running the business yourself, as the owner of a full-service wash or an exterior-conveyor wash, you'll first go into the "office" (most likely a small room at your wash) to coordinate the day's events. Based on a number of factors, including the weather, the season, and the day of the week, you'll have to make some decisions about the number of employees you'll need that day and when you'll need them. If you had planned on having only half a dozen employees in that day because the weatherman predicted rain, you'll have to round up some extra workers if it turns out to be bright and sunny. If the opposite happens—unexpected bad weather—you're going to have to reschedule some employees or find something else for them to do (if you're lucky, something that contributes to your sales).

The next task is to make sure that your equipment is operating as it should be. Is the machinery functioning properly? Do you have all of the necessary supplies? If you encounter a problem that you can't fix on your own, you'll have to find a repairperson—and fast—or risk losing significant business.

Once open, your day will probably be spent monitoring the wash. Some owners like to be very accessible to their customers, chatting up regulars and introducing themselves to new customers, building a bond so that they'll choose your wash over a competitor's.

There's a very good chance that you'll have to do some trouble-shooting as well. No matter how good your equipment and employees are, there are going to be problems during a typical day. There are some cars that a fully automated, exterior-conveyor wash just cannot clean to the owner's satisfaction. There are stories of owners with off-road vehicles, caked with mud and grime, visiting a car wash after a session of "four wheeling" and complaining that one run through the tunnel failed to clean the car. You, as the owner, are going to hear about it when something like that happens. Is there a scratch on the car that was clearly there before it ran through your wash, which the owner of the car blames you for anyway? These are all situations you'll encounter if not every day, at least on a regular basis. What you decide your customer service policy is going to be will in large part dictate how you interact with customers on a daily basis. Will it be "We're not satisfied until you're satisfied," or "We cannot be held responsible for damage to your car"?

Depending on how many employees you have, at the end of the day you may spend some time counting and distributing tips to your "send-off" employees (the people who dry off the car at the end of the cycle) or computing commissions for your service writers.

After everyone else has gone home, there's still some work left for you to do. (Hey, it's lonely at the top.) You're probably going to want to do a rundown of the day's business. Was it significantly more or less than you had expected? If it was significantly busier, you'll want to try to figure out why. Was it something you did, or was it luck? Was it some brilliant stroke of marketing genius? And speaking of marketing, how did your efforts pay off? How many coupons did you redeem today? Where did they come from? Did new customers redeem them, or are you just giving discounts to the regulars who come to you anyway?

If business was a bit slower than you expected, what can you do to improve? Assuming the weather was good and there weren't any other extenuating circumstances, there must have been some other problem, right? Maybe, maybe not. But it's almost a guarantee that you'll think about it long after everyone else is at home with their families.

After you're done analyzing the day's events, it's time to check the equipment and supplies again, and get ready for tomorrow. You may listen to the weather report to see if you're going to have to adjust your staffing to compensate for better- or worse-than-expected weather.

When all that's done, you're done. And you get to look forward to coming in bright and early the next day, and doing it all over again.

The Self-Serve Car Wash Owner

As the owner of a self-service or an in-bay-automatic car wash, you'll face some of the same challenges of a conveyor wash owner, but on a somewhat smaller scale. And some of the issues conveyor owners deal with, you won't have to worry about at all.

The typical day in the life of a self-serve owner is going to vary greatly depending on the size of your operation. We'll start by following the hypothetical owner of a mid-sized self-serve—a "3 and 1 combination," or a wash with three self-service bays and one in-bay automatic. Once you see what that's like, then we'll discuss what life is like for the car wash mogul—the owner with a large self-serve facility or one who has several washes dotted around town.

If you have a small operation, you may not have any employees. So that's one headache gone. But guess what, there's another one right there to take its place. If you have no employees, it's certainly true that just about everything involved in running a business is easier. Payroll's a snap (since it's nonexistent). Recordkeeping is much simpler, and there are a whole host of rules and regulations surrounding the hiring and firing of employees that you simply don't have to concern yourself with. But remember, all those things that employees would do if you had them now have to be done by you.

So how do you start your day? Here's a hint: You're probably not going to want to wear your nice shoes, because you're probably going to start your day cleaning up. Self-serve car washes, especially if they're open 24/7, get dirty. And people don't want to wash their cars at a dirty car wash.

There are lots of things that need to be cleaned at a self-serve wash. First and foremost are the bays themselves. Not surprisingly, when dirty cars get washed, they leave some dirt behind. You don't want your customers to take one look inside your bays and decide to go to the other car wash a mile away. One of your first duties of the day will be to wash down your bays. You may not have to clean your bays every

Doing Away with Graffiti

From time to time, you're probably going to walk into your wash and be greeted by graffiti. Even if your car wash is located in a peaceful, low-crime area, your bay walls are sometimes going to be defaced. Cleaning this stuff up is a hassle. Most hardware stores sell spray-on graffiti removers that you can buy. You can also try some other products, such as Klenztone, made by K&E Chemical Co. Inc. in Cleveland, which is supposed to work on brick.

One car wash owner in Southern California uses chlorine on his concrete walls to clean the grime and bacteria that tends to accumulate in most places that are wet all the time. For graffiti, this same owner has had some success using carburetor cleaner—available for probably less than two bucks at most hardware and auto supply stores. Other products that some owners have recommended are NU-Wall, made by Arcadian, and Clean-Up, made by Blue Coral. Keep trying various products until you find one that works best on your type and color of walls.

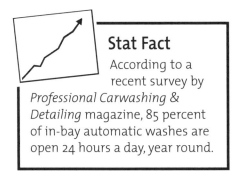

Stat Fact
According to a recent survey by *Professional Carwashing & Detailing* magazine, 85 percent of in-bay automatic washes are open 24 hours a day, year round.

day, but you should certainly expect to clean them once a week. You'll also probably have to deal with mold or mildew that will accumulate on your walls periodically.

After the bays are cleaned, you're going to have walk around your facility and pick up any miscellaneous garbage that might be lying around. One thing to keep in mind here is that the amount of garbage that's going to accumulate is going to vary depending on the number of vending machines you choose to install. (If you elect to supplement your sales in this way, see Chapter 9 for more information.) Empty soda cans or candy wrappers may be a nuisance, but considering the money you're going to be making from your vending machines, it's probably worth it.

Weather may not play as big a role in your day-to-day operations because, no matter if it's a sunny day or torrential rain, your operation can essentially remain open without incurring the added costs of employees standing around doing nothing. This assumes, of course, that you're managing the operation on your own. If, however, you have an employee whose job it is to remain at the wash, help customers with questions, or deal with complaints, then you will have to make some decisions about how much help you'll need on any given day.

The next thing you're going to have to do is collect your money. Theft is always a concern, and money left in the machines at your wash is bait for thieves. When you actually make the rounds to collect money, keep this guideline in mind: Most owners of self-serves advise against developing a routine or pattern that potential criminals can pick up on. For example, if you always show up at 8 A.M. to collect the money, someday you may find a thief waiting right behind you when you're finished.

Then, just like a conveyor owner would, you have to check your equipment and supplies. Because you probably aren't going to be on-site the entire time your wash is operational, you're going to have check for little things that may have gone wrong during the time you were away. Are all of the lights functional? Has a careless customer broken some minor piece of equipment? Are any cash machines or dispensers not working properly? These are the kinds of things you'll be looking for.

Finally, you'll have to do some routine maintenance if you haven't hired someone to do it for you. The exterior of your wash should be clean, well-lit and free of debris. If you own more than one location, you'll have to do the same routine all over again for each one. The instructions are similar to those on a bottle of shampoo—wash, rinse, and repeat.

Although it may sound like this is easier work than managing a full-service or exterior-conveyor wash, that's not always true. Some self-serve owners with lots of bays to take care of can wind up working harder and longer than their conveyor owner counterparts. But as a general rule, you can probably expect to spend a bit less time running a self-serve car wash business.

What Are Your Goals?

Which path you choose—the more relaxed structure of a self-serve wash or the more intense management of a conveyor wash—is entirely up to you. You may be constrained by start-up capital, which can be close to $1 million for a full-service car wash. As an alternative, you may be forced into the more modest expense of opening a few self-service bays. Bear in mind, however, that your goals have to play just as important a role in your decision as your financial ability to invest the capital.

We've mentioned before that you probably can't make a very comfortable living operating a few self-service bays and nothing else. This isn't the case with a complex wash that offers full-service treatment, detailing, lube jobs, oil changes, gasoline, a gift shop, and any number of services or products that help boost the bottom line. Keep that in mind if you plan to start small, it may be some time before you're able to truly quit your day job.

Safety and Cleanliness

There's no getting around the fact that you're going to have to spend some time every day paying attention to the cleanliness of your wash and any safety concerns that may arise. You'd be surprised just how dirty a place that's covered in soap and water all day long can get.

The worst offenders are often unattended self-service bays. Ask owners who have been in the business for any length of time, and they'll tell you stories about the guy who hosed down his manure-hauling pickup truck, for example. There are many people who don't think there's any problem at all washing whatever they happen to need washed in your bays, so get ready to start cleaning up after them—or suffer the consequences. We don't like to make too many guarantees, but we're pretty confident in saying that not too many customers are going to want to pull into a filthy car wash.

Along with cleanliness, safety always has to be paramount in your mind. With all that water around, it's important that you take

Stat Fact
OSHA inspected close to 700 car washes last year. Six percent of those inspections were prompted by a death or serious injury that occurred at the wash.

steps to guard against ice and slippery conditions, especially in colder climates. You and your employees will also be working with chemicals—some of which can be harmful. We're not talking so much about the materials used to clean cars, but some of the cleaning solutions you'll be forced to use on your bays to remove graffiti or mold and mildew. Make sure that you and your employees use these chemicals properly, and that you take the appropriate precautions to prevent any safety mishaps.

Beware!
Everything your customers touch needs to be inspected at least once a day. For example, if a careless customer smears grease on the nozzle of a vacuum, your next customer is going to get that grease all over her car's upholstery.

One of the consequences of not paying attention to safety and cleanliness can be a lawsuit. Here's an example of what can happen: A woman slipped and fell on some standing water at a car wash and claimed she injured her back. Of course, she decided to sue the owner. While that case was pending, another lawsuit was filed, this time by the woman's husband. It seems that the woman's back was hurt so badly, that the loving couple could no longer ... well, you know. The husband sued the car wash owner for "loss of affection" because of his wife's injury.

It sounds outrageous. It sounds silly. It sounds like it could never happen to you. But believe it or not, we heard this scenario from two owners who said that it happened to them. Think about that the next time you take chances about cleaning up water or other potential hazards.

Setting Up
Shop

Now that you have a good handle on just what to expect when running your business, you can start to make some educated decisions about how to set up your business. There are lots of things to consider: What form your business will take (i.e., corporation, sole proprietor, etc.); what experts to establish relationships with; what type of insurance you need; whether to buy, lease, or build your car wash; regulatory issues; naming your business; and writing your mission statement. Let's start with how to structure your business.

What Form Should Your Business Take?

Very early on in the process of starting your new car wash, you're going to have to make a decision about what form it should take. Will it be a sole proprietorship, corporation, limited liability company (LLC), etc.? For this decision, you're definitely going to need an accountant and probably a lawyer who can sit down with you and spell out the implications of each type of business structure, but here are some general points to consider.

If you incorporate, the general assumption is that you're shielding your personal assets from the risk of lawsuits. This means that if someone is injured on your property or sues you for something else that occurred in the process of washing a car on your property, the customers can only get the assets of the business itself. Generally speaking, the customer can't go after assets such as your personal savings account, your house, etc. Mark G., the car wash owner in Carson, California, incorporated right away, which is reportedly common in the industry. Mark chose an S corporation.

If there are advantages to incorporating, with those advantages come more paperwork, more record-keeping, and many more technical details to take care of—that's one reason you can't make this decision without some expert advice.

Many entrepreneurs wind up starting their businesses as a sole proprietorship or a partnership. Let's talk a little about these two business structures. One of the biggest advantages to forming as a sole proprietorship is that it's easy to do. Basically, the only work you're going to have to do is to obtain whatever general business licenses are required by your city or state to allow you to start doing business. This form of business structure is probably going to be the easiest for you to deal with when it comes time to pay your taxes. Generally, the income from the

> **Tip...**
>
> **Smart Tip**
>
> If you want your neighbors to see you as an upstanding member of the community, be sure to give something back. Consider donating money to the local Boy or Girl Scouts, or other community organizations. Or consider buying ads in local school newspapers or yearbooks. Not only will it help people remember your name, but it can also give you an edge in the community should you need to change, modify, or oppose regulations with the potential to hurt your business.

business is considered personal income, and you simply attach a Schedule C Form as part of a standard 1040 form. While there's less hassle involved, there's also a downside. With a sole proprietorship, you are the business. This means if someone slips and falls on a patch of ice in one of your wash bays, you're the one who's going to pay for it, not a faceless corporate entity. This could potentially raise your insurance costs.

If you're going into the business with a partner, you're probably going to need a partnership agreement. This is a little more complicated than a sole proprietorship, but is still easier to set up than a corporation. You get some of the same advantages with a partnership that you do with a sole proprietorship—ease of setup, no bureaucratic decision-making process, and a direct income from your business. However, there is a downside. At least one of you is still going to be completely personally liable for all the risks associated with a business. Another problem is that if one partner decides he wants out, there goes your partnership. You would then have to restructure the business as a sole proprietorship or find another partner. But perhaps the biggest disadvantage is that you generally have to stand by any agreements your partner makes. That can be dangerous if your partner isn't someone you completely trust.

As we said above, this really isn't a decision you should make without consulting an attorney who can take into account your particular circumstances and recommend the structure that's right for you.

The Experts

No man is an island. To give yourself the best chance of succeeding in your new business, you're going to need to establish relationships with a stable of experts—people you can call on to deal with situations that will inevitably arise in the course of doing business. Here are some of the professionals you'll need to consult at start-up, and potentially from time to time after that.

Legal Eagles

It should go without saying that you're going to need someone to handle your legal affairs. You should be able to perform more mundane tasks, such as getting a business license, but if you're ever sued, you certainly aren't going to be defending yourself in court. Your lawyer can also offer advice on how to set up your car wash to avoid potential legal conflicts and can advise you on the form of business (sole proprietorship, corporation, etc.) that would be best for you. To find a qualified attorney, start with the American Bar Association (www.aba.org) or your local city, or state's bar association.

Number-Crunchers

You don't necessarily need an accountant, but it certainly wouldn't be a bad idea. When you own your own business, your taxes are going to become more complicated really fast. A reliable accountant handling these things frees you up to focus on growing your business. An accountant can also help you find ways to reduce those taxes and help you keep on track with your business budget. There are several places you can check to find an accountant you're comfortable with. Try the National Association of Small Business Accountants (www.smallbiz accounts.com), the American Institute of Certified Public Accountants (www.aicpa.org), and the National Association of Insurance and Financial Advisors (www.naifa.org). See the Appendix for additional contact information.

Stat Fact
According to a recent report from the International Carwash Association, 76 percent of full-service car wash owners have a gift shop as an added profit center.

Insurance Agents

Having an insurance expert who takes the time to understand your particular situation and develops a plan that gives you the right coverage without selling you policies you don't need, is vital. Don't even think about opening without first consulting an insurance professional. You can start your search at the Independent Insurance Agents of America (www.iiaa.org) or the National Association of Professional Insurance Agents (www.pianet.com).

Repairpersons

Because so much of your business relies on keeping all that machinery up and running, you're going to need a capable repairperson to handle problems if you can't. The distributor who sold you your equipment might be a good place to start looking for one, as that company will often service the equipment it sells you. If you're buying an existing car wash, you might want to stick with the same person the previous owner used, since he or she will probably know the equipment inside and out.

Fun Fact
Did you know that when you buy your car wash you'll be a colleague of Lenny Dykstra, the former Philadelphia Phillies' and New York Mets' great? Dykstra owns a car wash chain.

Architects

You're only going to need an architect if you're building a brand-new wash or are planning extensive renovations to an existing structure. Obviously, not every architect is going to be the right person to design a car wash, so you may have to do some searching. Ask fellow owners if they can recommend someone or check with an organization such as The National Council of Architectural Registration Boards (www.ncarb.org) to find information on licensed architects in your state. Your distributor, supplier, and equipment manufacturer can also probably recommend a qualified professional with car wash experience.

Insurance Issues

As we said above, you can't go into business without insurance. Here are some of the things your insurance policy should cover:

- *Your building and its contents.* Coverage should pay to replace any loss of your car wash and equipment.
- *Loss of business income.* If a disaster happens and you need to close your wash for an extended period of time, you're going to need insurance to recoup your losses.
- *Equipment breakdown.* In addition to insurance coverage that protects you in case your equipment is destroyed, you should also look for coverage in case your equipment simply breaks down.
- *General liability.* This is insurance that protects you against lawsuits, injury claims, damage claims, etc.
- *Workers' compensation.* If you have employees, you should carry coverage that protects you against injuries to your workers.

You may decide on more coverage, but those are the basics. Your local car wash association may also have some sort of group insurance arrangement as part of its membership benefits, so you might want to look into that possibility, too. You can also check out the Insuracenter (www.carwashinsurance.com), a company that specializes in insuring car washes.

Should You Buy or Build Your Car Wash?

For a novice car wash owner, we'll go out on a limb here and say it's probably going to be easier for you to buy an existing car wash than to build a new one from the ground up. Why? One reason is that an existing business is somewhat of a known entity. You know how much revenue the business takes in every year. You know what the costs of operation are. In addition, customers already know that the business exists. Mark G. bought an existing business, as did Dick H., the car wash owner in Sacramento, California. Entrepreneur Richard K., in Chicago, also bought

Beware!

When buying an existing wash, ask to see revenue statements from at least the past three years. Never, ever accept as proof of revenue what the current owner claims are "representative" months. They could be the best months the wash has ever had.

an existing business, but he did some remodeling to expand and update the car wash.

Of course, some of these factors might change once you take over. If the previous owner never did a good job at marketing the business, you might be able to increase sales. If he never paid much attention to costs, you might be able to streamline the business and increase your profits. But generally speaking, you pretty much know what you're getting.

Buying is also less complicated because you have less to worry about. There are no architects, no construction plans, no building permits, and (perhaps most important) no lag between the time you buy the business and when you actually start operating. All of the entrepreneurs interviewed for this book bought an existing facility, with the exception of one owner who expanded a self-service business into a self-service plus one in-bay automatic unit.

There are really only a few reasons you might want to start from scratch. One would be if the community lacks adequate car wash facilities. Another would be if the existing facilities are so run-down that what's available just simply isn't worth the price. If this is the case and you decide to build one, you'll have several more issues to think about.

Should You Lease or Buy Your Land?

One of the questions you're probably going to face if you decide to open a new car wash is whether to lease or buy your land. There are many factors that will come into play as you make this decision, and while most people would argue that it's better to own the land, some differ over which option is better. Most owners you talk to will say that it's better to own the land your car wash is on rather than lease it. But in some cases, it may be impossible to buy the land. Perhaps the parcel you've targeted for your business isn't for sale. Perhaps you're not a good candidate to buy the land, either because you lack the required capital to purchase it outright or lending companies aren't willing to lend you enough money to make the purchase and build your wash. In short, there might be any number of reasons—some, which may be up to you, others that may not—leasing makes a lot of sense. First, let's talk a little about how much land you're going to need.

The Size of Your Lot

Before you decide what land to buy, you need to know how much land is required for the type of car wash you want to open. Equipment manufacturer Dultmeier Sales recommends a rule of thumb that says your lot should be 100 feet to 120 feet deep and a minimum of 75 feet wide. Again, these are minimums. If you want to open a four-bay wash, you should look for a lot that's at least 100 feet wide.

For a conveyor system, you're generally going to need a lot about 60 feet longer than the length of your equipment. These dimensions may vary depending on the layout of your car wash. An experienced car wash architect can help you determine exactly how much space you'll need. Now let's get back to the topic of acquiring land.

Lose Your Lease, Lose Your Wash

One of the biggest arguments against leasing is that there is always the danger, if you aren't careful to construct the lease in terms that are favorable to you, that you could lose your wash when your lease expires. Should the owner of the land decide not to renew your lease, you'll be permitted to take all your equipment, but the money you spent constructing the building will be lost. While that's certainly an extreme danger and one serious enough to have caused many owners to absolutely swear off leasing as an option, there are some ways you can insulate yourself against this possibility.

Always Push for Long Lease Terms

Obviously, if you lease your land from year to year as opposed to having a ten-year lease, you're in much greater jeopardy of losing your business at the whim of the landowner. This is one of the major reasons you want to negotiate as long a lease term as possible. It also insulates you against sudden upswings in the cost of land. If, for example, you're operating on a year-to-year lease, you can't really say with any accuracy what your land costs are going to be in any given year. Assuming that the owner won't kick you off the property to make room for a higher-paying tenant, you may still have to deal with wildly fluctuating rental costs. If the change is dramatic enough, it could make a once-profitable wash a prime candidate for bankruptcy.

Options to Renew

Another way to protect your business from the whims of the landowner is to negotiate for an option, or options, to renew. Essentially this means that, once your lease is up, you have the option to renew it for a certain period of time at a previously agreed upon rate. For example, if you have an initial lease period of ten years, with two options to renew for seven years each, you have essentially secured your rights to use the land for 24 years (ten years on the initial agreement, plus seven years on the first renewal and seven more on the second renewal). Not only do you know that your building won't be taken away, but you can also determine with relative accuracy what your land costs are going to be.

What's a Good Lease Price?

The answer to this question depends on several factors. How big is the lot? How many bays, or what size car wash can it accommodate? How desirable is the location? In general, what constitutes a fair lease price will be determined by the size car wash the land can support. For example, land that will support a building large enough to accommodate a six-bay, self-service car wash will be worth more than a smaller parcel that will only accommodate a four-bay unit. Using the same logic, land that is perfectly situated in a prime, wash-friendly location is going to be worth more (at least to you) than a similarly sized parcel in a less desirable location.

Stat Fact
According to a recent survey by *Professional Carwashing & Detailing* magazine, more than 50 percent of exterior-conveyor washes currently operating were built before 1986.

There are no hard and fast rules about what you should pay to lease your land, but here are some guidelines. According to an *Auto Laundry News* survey, rent, on average, was about 15.5 percent of gross revenues for full-service and exterior-conveyor washes. In other words, after you've determined or estimated what you can reasonably expect to make from a car wash built on a particular parcel of land, you should probably try to avoid paying more than about 15.5 percent of that amount to rent the space.

As an example, let's take a look at an exterior-conveyor wash to see how this works. An exterior-conveyor car wash servicing 50,000 cars a year and averaging around $5.50 in gross revenue a car, will have projected annual revenue of $275,000. To figure out what an acceptable lease agreement would be in order to make this a viable proposition, we first calculate 15.5 percent of $275,000. This comes to $42,625. Now divide that by 12 to determine a fair monthly rate, and you get about $3,552.

Of course, that's not a price you can live with if you're operating a much smaller business—such as a three-bay, self-service car wash that may only generate around $55,000 in gross annual revenue. In that instance, you're looking for land that will cost in the range of $710 a month to lease.

Stat Fact
You don't have to be a car wash mogul to make it. Seventy-one percent of self-service car wash owners have just one location, says a recent survey in *Auto Laundry News.*

Use these figures for what they are—guidelines. There are undoubtedly washes that pay more for land and succeed, just as there are undoubtedly washes that pay less than that and fail. But at least by knowing some general numbers, you'll be able to tell if your business is doomed before it ever gets off the ground or if you've stumbled upon a truly sweet deal.

Other Lease Factors

In addition to those provisions we've already mentioned, there are some other things you might want to look for in a lease. One of those might be an option to buy the land out-

Smart Tip

What's the best car wash investment? Some experts say it's a wash that's in a good location but that hasn't been cared for. With a little elbow grease, you can revamp the site and capitalize on the great location.

right at some future date, or at least a right-of-first-refusal should the current owner decide to sell. Although it's probably very unlikely that you'll be able to get a purchase option, it's slightly more plausible that an owner will agree to a right-of-first-refusal clause. The value of these and the other provisions (such as an option to renew) is that they protect you should situations change unexpectedly. Because you don't own the land, you should be making every attempt to insulate yourself and your business from a leasing disaster. It might seem like an extra headache, but it's not too far off-base to say that taking the time to investigate these provisions could mean the difference in whether or not you'll still have a car wash business five or ten years from now.

Buying Your Land

While leasing might seem complicated, buying isn't exactly a walk in the park, either. Sure, you don't have to worry that a landlord will suddenly pull the rug out from under your feet and rent your land to a new fast-food restaurant, but buying land requires that you have more capital at your disposal for one thing. In some cases, this one factor might make the decision for you, and you'll wind up leasing because of it.

If you're considering buying the land, it's a good idea to hire a real estate agent who can help you through the process. You might also want to contact car wash experts to evaluate a site before you put down any money.

Regulatory Issues

The licenses and permits you'll need to operate your wash are going to vary according to your local laws and regulations. You should be in contact with your local government or chamber of commerce to decide which licenses you'll need, but in general, you can expect to have to obtain a business license from your town or city. Because you're operating a car wash, you might also need permits that cover water use and/or

Slow It Down

Corner lots are usually great locations for just about any type of business, especially if cars have access to your location from two streets. But there is a downside to what would be an otherwise great location. Americans are an impatient bunch, and judging from the way some people drive, there's nothing we hate more than sitting in traffic or waiting at stoplights. Some anxious drivers might see your lot as a convenient shortcut to bypass traffic. This isn't just annoying; it can be dangerous, too. With customers moving around and cars pulling in and out of wash or vacuum bays, all it takes is one careless driver to ram headlong into an unsuspecting customer or car.

When you're setting up your lot, consider adding speed bumps to force cars to slow down. If you're lucky enough to be on a corner, you might also want to think about installing signs that discourage drivers from using your business as a way to avoid normal traffic delays.

Stat Fact
According to a recent study from the International Carwash Association, nearly 85 percent of consumers agree with the statement: "Having a clean car makes me feel good."

pollution and environmental contamination. If you plan on constructing extensive signage, you'll have to check local zoning ordinances to find out the size and location of signage that's permitted.

If you add offline services such as oil changes, gas sales, propane sales, a gift shop, or food service, you'll probably need additional permits. You should work with your lawyer, who can help make sure you're in total compliance with your local government's regulations.

Testing the Waters

As a car wash owner, water is something you're going to come to know a lot about. One of the reasons is that the makeup of your water is going to determine, at least to a certain extent, how well you can wash cars. Another reason is that it's going to affect how customers perceive your wash. (We'll explain that one in a minute.) Finally, the government is going to want to know something about your water as well.

Let's start with how the chemistry of your water affects the quality of the service you provide. What you're concerned with here is how soft or hard your water is. The key thing to remember here is that you want soft water. Depending on where you live, that may require a water-softening system. Some places of the country, like Los Angeles, have car wash owners who refer to their water as liquid rock—meaning it's incredibly hard and requires treatment to make it up to snuff for car wash standards.

Local pool-supply stores or water-treatment facilities sell kits that allow you to test your water and determine its level of hardness or softness. You can also ask your water company to do an analysis. The level of hardness or softness is measured in something called "grains." Zero grains hardness is the best for our purposes. Anything between zero and five grains, and you might be able to get by without a softening system. Anything more than five, and you're dealing with liquid rock.

Here's why this is so important: Detergents work best at zero grains hardness. In other words, the soap you use, no matter what soap that is, is going to clean cars better when your water is soft. A second, equally important reason for using soft water is your equipment. Hard water taxes your equipment much more than soft water does, meaning there's more wear and tear, more breakdowns, more repair costs, and ultimately a shorter life span for the lifeblood of your business.

Soft water is also important in how customers perceive your business. It may sound strange. After all, hard water is something you can't see. It looks just like soft water. It doesn't smell any different than soft water, nor does it taste different. So what difference does it make to your customers if your water is hard or soft? In a word, "bubbles." Your customers like to see bubbles and foam when they drive through your wash. It makes them feel good, like there's really something powerful going on to get the dirt and grime off their cars. Soap foams much better when the water isn't hard. Soft water will also allow you to use less soap, because hard water requires more soap be used to achieve the same level of foaminess.

Assuming that you do need to soften your water, you're going to need equipment to do that. These systems will usually consist of two tanks that work together to soften the water. It's going to require some maintenance and monitoring on your part to make the system function properly. The manufacturer of your system, or the distributor who sold it to you, should be able to provide a complete explanation of how it works and what your responsibilities are in keeping it working.

Here are some ground rules to keep in mind. Your system should be big enough to handle the volume of business your wash does. Anyone who's ever tried to take a hot shower in a house filled with people with an undersized water tank will probably tell you to err on the safe side. What this means is that you should get something that's perhaps slightly larger than you think you might need on an average day. Second, owners without the knowledge of how a water softening system works don't realize that their equipment may be "regenerating"—essentially flushing itself out—at the wrong time of day. You want this to occur at a time when your car wash is either closed or, if you're running a 24-hour self-service wash, when it's not busy (maybe something like 2 A.M. or 3 A.M. if this is the case).

Environmental Studies

Another reason you have to worry about your water is that the water going out of your car wash matters to regulatory agencies. There are a number of environmental concerns your local city-planning department is likely to have. These could include: surface water run-off, waste-water discharge, oil and/or sludge disposal, and water recycling, to name a few. You should consult the local government in your area to ask for information on the regulations regarding water use and recycling. You may be required to install things such as sand traps to filter out any sludge that's mixed in with your water, before it reaches the sewer drain.

> **Tip...**
>
> **Smart Tip**
>
> It's important to educate your customers to dispel some of the common myths about the car washing process. According to the International Carwash Association, nearly half the owners of conveyor washes (including full-service and exterior-conveyor) provide reprints of articles about car washing to their customers and give information about water recycling and environmental benefits.

To protect your business, you might want to do a Phase I Environmental Study, which should cost around $2,000. This will help determine, before you ever take possession of a car wash, what environmental damage has already been done to the surrounding area. It's kind of like a walk-through you'd do before taking possession of an apartment or house. You don't want to be held responsible for damage that the previous owner may have caused. If you finance the purchase of an existing wash, your lender may require an environmental study. To find a reputable professional who can conduct an environmental study for your business, ask any industry associations you join for referrals.

Naming Your Car Wash

We'll talk a bit more about this in Chapter 10, on marketing and public relations, but for now you should start thinking about what you want to name your car wash. You can get creative and start dreaming up names like "Suds Are Us" or "Slick Willie's" if you want. That's fine. But all the experts say that, no matter what you decide on for a name, the words "car wash" need to be in there.

Try coming up with a name that clearly tells people where your car wash is located, or at least the general area. "Parkside Car Wash" or "Center Street Car Wash" are just a couple of examples. Another alternative is to choose a name that represents the service you ideally want to provide—like "Clean and Convenient Car Wash" or "Speedy

Car Wash." Yet another consideration is including the type of car wash you have ("Jerry's Full-Service Car Wash" or "Broadway Self-Service Car Wash," for example).

Writing Your Mission Statement

Your mission statement is going to define your reasons for being in business. It should contain language that will help you and your employees understand how the day-to-day operations of your business will be run.

In essence, your mission statement will be the vision for your business. Once you have this worked out, you can start to make all the other little decisions involved in starting and running a business, based on how closely they match with your overall philosophy. For example, if your mission statement says something to the effect of "Our goal is to provide the best possible wash at the lowest possible price," that will help dictate the decisions you make in everything from your pricing structure and menu of services to the amount of soap you use during your wash cycle.

Specifically, what kinds of things should your mission statement contain? Here are a few ideas:

- *Philosophy*. Don't worry. You don't have to be Socrates to come up with a winning philosophy about how to run a car wash. This doesn't have to be long; it just has to convey what you see as "the big picture." Think of it this way: What one sentence would you like your customers to say when a friend asks them "Hey, what's that new car wash down on the corner like?" When you start coming up with answers, that's a good start toward developing a real philosophy.

- *Customer service policy*. Are you going to take the attitude that "The customer is always right?" Or are you determined to take a hard-line stance against the customer who claims you scratched his car, when you know darn well it wasn't your fault? Make sure that, whatever tack you decide to take, you actually follow through when customers start coming to your car wash. Words don't mean anything if your actions don't back them up.

- *Pricing policy*. It's easy to say that you want to be the cheapest wash in town, but there's more to a pricing policy than that. Remember, the cheapest wash isn't always the best wash, nor is it always the wash that has the most customers and makes the most money. Maybe you want to say that your prices will be "fair" or "competitive" instead. If you're determined to build the Rolls Royce of car washes, maybe your policy is going to be that customers will have to pay the most to get the best.

- *Employee policy*. This should really cover three things: the treatment your employees can expect from you, the treatment you expect from them, and the treatment your customers deserve. If you make it clear what kind of behavior you expect from your employees at the outset, it will be much easier, both for them and for you, to maintain a standard of excellence in your business.

- *Damage policy.* This kind of goes hand-in-hand with your customer service policy, but it still makes sense to spell it out explicitly. What's the general attitude you're going to take when someone claims that you've damaged his or her car? That's the question you want to answer here. You have two choices. You can come at it from the attitude that you'll do whatever you can to make things right, or you can take the view that damage isn't your responsibility. There's some gray area between those two ends of the spectrum, and you may choose to strike a compromise, but in general, you'll find that your idealized statement will fall into one of the former two categories.

That's about it for areas that you really have to cover. You'll probably put in additional language based on your unique situation, and that's fine. One thing to keep in mind, though, is that you want the statement to be relatively short—something people can read in a few minutes. Anything longer than that, and you're probably being overly specific.

Start-Up
Expenses

Now we're going to give you the solid financial information you'll need to determine the type of wash that's right for you, based on the capital you have available (or at least have access to).

The good thing about the car wash business is that it can accommodate many different types of owners—

from someone who wants a small side business to someone who's ready to enter the industry and make it their sole source of income. If you're the side-business type, you can probably get in with a small self-service wash for just over $100,000. If you want the kind of operation that's going to provide you with a nice return on your investment, then you're going to have to come up with about four times that or more.

If you're buying an existing wash, well then obviously the start-up expense is going to be the price you pay (or at least the down payment), plus any miscellaneous legal fees or bank fees that go along with it. Trying to tell you what your start-up expenses will be in this case is a little like trying to tell someone how much it costs to buy a house. You can't do it. It depends on the size of the house, the location, the age, and a host of other factors. Car washes are the same way.

With that said, there are certainly ways to tell if you're getting a good deal. Review the discussion on how to determine a rate of return in Chapter 9. This will give you a good indication of whether the rewards you can expect from a particular wash justify the risks.

Another method would be to look at a figure called the gross income multiplier (GIM). A rough estimate of a "good" multiplier might be anywhere from 2.5 to 3.5. What this means is that you can safely pay 2.5 times to 3.5 times the gross annual revenue of a wash and still be getting a decent deal. In other words, if a wash does $150,000 a year in gross revenues, you should expect to pay between $375,000 and $525,000 for the business. Again, this is a rough guideline, but it can prevent you from overpaying for a site or alert you when you may be getting a steal.

If you build a new business, the largest costs are going to be for the land, structure, and the equipment itself. Let's start by looking at some sample costs for a few different kinds of washes (see the charts on pages 74–77). In the examples provided, we've assumed that you're either buying an existing business or building a new wash and leasing the land. If you decide to purchase the land instead, your start-up costs would look a bit different.

Where the Money Goes

Your largest expense initially is going to be acquiring land and equipping it with your washing machinery or acquiring an existing business. But running a car wash is like running any other business. There are a host of other little odds and ends that can add up—and quickly. See the "Equipment Checklist" on pages 56 and 57 for an idea of what typical equipment expenses look like for both full- and self-service washes.

One of the advantages to buying an existing wash is that you'll probably be buying many of these things (fax machines, phones, computers, etc.) along with it. But let's assume you don't inherit the equipment or that you need to supplement the equipment that you've acquired with an existing business. What will you need?

The list of equipment you're going to need will vary depending on the type of car wash you'll be starting. For example, while the owner of a full-service wash is going to need a cash register, a self-serve owner won't. But you will need a bill changer instead.

Office Equipment and Supplies

To start, let's tackle the items that are pretty much going to be common to all car washes, regardless of their size or the market they serve.

Computer System

Depending on what you're going to be using the computer for—simple record-keeping or database marketing, for example—you may be able to get away with a simple, inexpensive system for around $1,500. However, if you plan to do advanced database marketing, or just want to go with a higher-end model, then you're talking about something over $2,000. You probably aren't going to need anything more than that.

What should you look for in a computer system? Here are some minimum requirements you should check for:

- *Pentium-class processor*
- *Current version of Microsoft Windows*
- *64MB RAM*
- *8GB to 10GB hard drive*
- *CD-ROM drive (24X or faster)*
- *56Kbps modem*

A computer meeting these standards should be able to handle anything you, as a car wash owner, will be likely to need. Of course, there are all types of bells and whistles you can get to go along with the basics, such as a drive that will allow you to record your own CDs. But unless you plan on keeping your customers entertained with custom music CDs in the waiting room or want to store records on a data CD rather than on your hard drive or a floppy disk, it probably doesn't make much sense to spend the extra cash.

Computer Peripherals

One "extra" you are going to want is a printer. Here, too, it's possible to break the bank on the latest model. In all seriousness, think about what you're going to be using your printer for—printing fliers, signs, employee manuals, memos, etc. The reason

▲

Equipment Checklist

Here are the equipment and supplies that you'll need or want to have. We've provided a high-end estimate for a full-service car wash and low-end estimate for a self-service car wash with two wash bays. Both scenarios assume that you are building a new business and will need to acquire equipment.

Keep in mind that your equipment costs will vary depending on whether you decide to buy an existing wash (which should come with much of the equipment you'll need) or build from scratch (in which case you'll need to buy the equipment you need to get started). And remember, it is possible to build a car wash without some of the equipment listed below. These costs are general guidelines for what you can expect to pay.

Equipment	Full-Service	Self-Service
Wash-Related Equipment		
Power-wash units	$225,000 (1 unit)	$30,000 (2 units)
Vacuums	10,000 (10 units)	2,000 (2 units)
Automatic dryers (conveyor systems only)	15,000 (1 unit)	0
Water heater	4,000	2,000
Water reclamation/recycling	25,000	15,000
Water softener	6,000	4,000
Retail/Lot Equipment		
Shaded vacuum area	$3,500	$0
Floor heater	0	3,000
Vending machines	1,500 (1 unit)	0 (if offered free by distributor such as Coke or Pepsi)

you want to think about it is because you have a couple of choices here. The first is to go with the old standby—a black-and-white laser printer. This will print much sharper images than its inkjet counterparts and only cost a bit more (probably less than $1,000 for a basic model). So if you're satisfied living without color, this is probably the way to go.

The other option you have is to go full color. The price of a color laser printer is probably going to make this option impractical, unless, of course, you have money to

Equipment Checklist, continued

Equipment	Full-Service	Self-Service
Change machines	$1,500 (2 units)	$750 (1 unit)
Signage	10,000	1,000
Security system	5,000	100
Landscaping	500	200
Trash receptacles	500	50
Bathroom fixtures	750	0 (assuming you don't provide facilities)
Cash register	3,000	0
Lighting (exterior)	1,500	500
Inventory	10,000	0
Office Equipment		
Furniture	$1,500	$300
Computer	3,000	1,000
Computer software	1,000	100
Printer	1,000	200
Phone system	500	100
Fax machine	700 (Multifunction machine)	200
Paper shredder	300	25
Calculator	50	15
Total	**$330,800**	**$60,540**

burn. Instead, you're likely going to be looking at a color inkjet that's going to give you some nice options in terms of color output, but that's going to produce text that's a bit less clear when you compare it to a laser printer. Plan on spending in the range of $250 to $500 for a color inkjet printer.

The choice is up to you. If you plan to use your computer and printer to create signs for your customers and employees, then you may want to look into the color option. If memos and spreadsheets are your thing, then a laser printer is probably better.

▲

Software

This is another one of those areas that can get dicey. Visit any office supply shop and you'll no doubt find dozens of software packages that you think will help you run your business more effectively. Of course, they might also put you out of business once you wind up paying for all of them.

You can go off the deep end here and wind up spending a lot more than you really have to. To start, it's a good idea to just stick with the essentials. You're going to need an accounting program, such as Microsoft Money or Intuit QuickBooks ($80 to $250); a basic word processing program, such as Microsoft Word or Corel WordPerfect ($85 to $250); and perhaps some type of desktop publishing program. You don't need to go overboard with that last one (some professional packages can cost up to $1,000). You simply need something that will allow you to print fliers or other simple signs. Figure on spending around $50 for something like Broderbund's Print Shop Deluxe, and that should get the job done.

If you're planning to compile a mailing list, you're going to need software to handle that, too. Microsoft Office (about $500) integrates several programs in one easy package: Word, for word processing; Excel, for creating spreadsheets; PowerPoint, for graphical presentations; and Publisher, for creating simple fliers, cards, brochures, etc. This may be a good option for you, since it includes tools that allow you to maintain mailing lists and merge your names with mailings you can compose right on Microsoft Word software. There are also stand-alone programs such as Parsons Technology's Ultimate Mail Manager that you can pick up for around $60.

Phone System

You're going to be on the phone quite regularly between ordering supplies, calling maintenance crews, and staffing your shifts, so you're going to need a decent system.

On the other hand, you aren't in the business of telemarketing, so breaking the bank isn't going to be necessary.

Depending on the size of your car wash, you're probably going to want at least two lines. If you opt for a fax machine, figure on three lines. Phone line installation will run you in the neighborhood of $40 to $60 a line. Plan on spending in the range of $70 to $150 for a two-line speakerphone with auto-redial, memory dial, mute button, and other goodies. You're also going to

Bright Idea

Need help convincing politicians or customers that your wash is environmentally friendly? Tell them about a book called *50 Simple Ways to Save the Earth* (published for the first Earth Day). The authors say that a self-service car wash is the most water-efficient way to wash a car.

want to get a pager (approximately $50 a year) so you can be reached at any time of the day or night in case of an emergency, as well as voice mail ($6 to $20 a month) or an answering machine ($35 to $65 for a basic model; $125 to $200 for one with advanced features). The goal here is simply to make sure that you can be reached whenever you're needed, and that you can reach your employees, your vendors, and your customers. Whatever it takes to accomplish that will do the trick, even if you don't opt for a system with all the bells and whistles the gadget-freak inside of you is longing for.

Miscellaneous Office Equipment

If you have a computer and a printer, you aren't going to need anything as old-fashioned as a typewriter. But you are going to need things such as a fax machine, calculator, and cash register (unless you run a self-serve car wash, in which case you can forget about the cash register). You may also want to invest in equipment, such as a paper shredder (yes, people will go through your garbage looking for goodies such as social security numbers or bank account statements) and a photocopier.

Let's talk first about cash registers. Everyone's seen those old movies where everything bought in-store was rung up on one of those old mechanical registers (and a few of us probably even remember them firsthand). But if you haven't been in business and had need for a cash register over the past 40 years or so, you'd be amazed at how far they've come. Your basic electronic cash register is going to run you anywhere from $600 to $3,000. And it gets worse. Let's say you want a point-of-sale (POS) system that is conveniently networked to your computer system. You're going to pay through the nose for that convenience—anywhere from $1,200 to $5,000 a terminal. Is it worth it? Probably not, unless you have an extensive gift shop or some other offline services you're providing. The basic car wash, even if it does include a small gift or accessories shop, can get by with a basic electronic model.

A paper shredder is a piece of cake to pick up at just about any office supply store (for about $25). Something in this price range is for light-duty use. It will probably handle around five sheets or so at once and is really intended for a home-office type of user who isn't going to be shredding phone books every day. If that's not good enough for you, you can look into a more substantial shredder that can handle just about anything you throw at it. You probably won't be surprised to hear that the price takes a big jump once you go beyond the small, over-the-trash-can type of shredder. Heavy-duty shredders go for between $150 and $500.

Fax machines are a little bit easier to get a handle on, but before we get to them, there's one possibility you may want to keep in mind. Assuming you took our advice and got a computer with a nice big hard drive and a speedy modem, you might be able to use that as a fax instead of buying an entirely new machine. Chances are your system came with some sort of fax software preinstalled. You

59

should be able to send and receive faxes, view them on your computer monitor, and print them out if you wish. It sounds like a great deal, and it may very well be, depending on what you plan to use the fax for. If you want to fax a hard copy of something, you can't unless you have a scanner (around $150 for a basic model). And even if you do have a scanner, it's certainly a waste of time to first scan a document and then fax it (it's really like faxing it twice—once to your computer, then once to the actual fax recipient). It might work for you if you plan to need a fax only on very rare occasions. Everyone else should probably bite the bullet and buy a dedicated machine.

If you're going for a basic fax machine, you have two choices: a plain-paper machine or a thermal machine. Plain paper is exactly what it sounds like; it prints out on normal copier or printer paper. The thermal-type machines use special rolls of paper and essentially burn the image onto the paper. They're a bit cheaper than the plain-paper faxes, and if you've ever used one you know why. They're a hassle. The pages curl, they can smudge, they're hard to file, and basically aren't worth the savings. A standard plain-paper model will sell for around $100 to $250.

There's also another choice, and that's to get a device that handles everything. And by everything, we mean everything. There are machines on the market today that can act as a printer, fax, copier, and scanner. If you shop around a bit, you might find that one of these multifunction machines could wind up saving you money. Of course, it makes no sense to get one that also functions as a scanner if you have no conceivable need for a scanner (other than to be the coolest car wash owner on the block). In any event, these machines go for between $250 and $800.

Office Furniture

Again, this cost will vary depending on the type of car wash you own. If you own a self-serve, there's probably a better than even chance that your office will be located off-site, perhaps even in your home, and you may be able to get away with using what you already have. If, however, you're equipping an office at your wash, there are a few things you're going to need.

Most car wash owners would never think about being elaborate with their office space, assuming that they even have office space that's not a spare bedroom or den. That's one of the nice things about this business—you're certainly not going to spend a majority of your time being a paper pusher. Figure on a desk, chair, and filing cabinet as the main expenses in equipping your office. You can probably get by spending less than $400 for these items. Then throw in miscellaneous office supplies such as paper, fax cartridges, floppy disks, folders, staples, paper clips, and what have you, and you're still talking less than $500, if you spend wisely. Not bad. (That's probably just about all you'll be able to afford anyway after the real equipment—your washing equipment—is taken care of.)

Wash-Related Equipment

Of all the decisions you make in starting your new wash, this is going to be one of the most important. The supplier you choose and the equipment you buy will probably impact your business for the next 15 to 20 years. It will also be a factor in the price of your wash if you decide to sell it at some point down the road.

With a decision this monumental, you'd probably like us to give you some definite answers about exactly which systems to buy and which manufacturer to use. Most manufacturers today produce quality equipment, and the one you choose to go with will probably have less of an impact on your business than one other very important factor—your local distributor.

Why is this so important? The manufacturer is not the one you're going to call if you have a problem that needs fixing ASAP. You're going to call the person who actually sold, delivered, and installed your system. If that person is unreliable or is located two hours away, you're going to have problems.

Establishing a Relationship with Your Distributor

Your decision on which equipment to buy should basically be driven by how you feel about working with the various distributors. If you're choosing between two different pieces of equipment, both of which are suitable for the services you want to provide, go with the better distributor (assuming the prices are comparable).

When we say "better distributor," that might mean different things to different people. So here are some specific things you should look for:

- *The distributor is located close by.* Generally, you're going to want to stay away from a distributor that is located in an area that's going to make it difficult for him to get to you quickly and easily if there's a problem. Some owners have chosen specific distributors simply because their offices were close by, while a competitor's was a couple of hours away, even though that second distributor's equipment was a tad better.

- *The distributor has been in business for a long time.* It's pretty hard to stay in business for any length of time if you're not good at what you do. Some distributors are family-owned businesses, passed down from generation to generation, indicating that they have a record of satisfying customers and that they aren't planning to go out of business any time soon. We're not saying that new distributors should be dismissed out of hand, but you certainly can't beat the comfort level that comes with a long track record.

- *The distributor provides references.* There's a fairly obvious element to this: A distributor with a long list of references to provide is more desirable than one who, for one reason or another, can't provide you with the names of any of his customers. You want to ask for references so that you can see what type of experience a prospective distributor has, as well as his track record for serving customers. Not so obvious is that a distributor should, if you ask, be willing to tell you the truth about customers who haven't been happy. Anyone who has been in business for any length of time is going to have had at least one customer who was unsatisfied. If the distributor is candid with you about an account they lost or a customer who was unhappy, it may provide insight into whether he is the best distributor for the type of car wash you plan to open.

- *The distributor knows your type of business.* It can help if the person you're dealing with has experience working with the type of car wash you plan to operate. For example, if the only car washes a prospective distributor has ever worked with are self-serves, he may not be the best choice if you have your sights set on a full-service wash.

New vs. Used Equipment

Car wash equipment isn't cheap, so we should probably spend some time talking about how to make good buying decisions. Properly cared for, your wash-related equipment should last a very long time (perhaps 20 years or so), but it's still a major investment that you're going to have to live with one way or the other.

Some new owners like the idea of buying used equipment as a way to cut their start-up costs. This can be a cost savings, or it can come back to haunt you. By all means, if you can find quality equipment that has been well maintained and is relatively new, you certainly could save yourself a bundle by outfitting your new wash with at least some used equipment. If you're thinking about going this route, consider the factors listed below carefully:

- *Service.* Will you have someone you can call if the equipment breaks down? When you buy new equipment, you're also getting a distributor who services it. When you buy used equipment, you might not. In the long run, if you have to pay extra to have the equipment serviced, it may turn out that it actually becomes more expensive to buy used equipment.

- *Maintenance.* As with any piece of machinery, car wash equipment will last longer when it's properly maintained. Before

Beware!
Before committing to any kind of vendor, do a search on the Internet for "business background checks." This will take you to a number of sites where you can find information on the legal history of a company you're thinking about purchasing from. If you find negative information, like a plethora of lawsuits, you'll probably want to avoid doing business with them.

making any kind of investment in used equipment, you should ask to see the maintenance records. What you're looking for is basically the same kind of stuff you'd be looking for if you were buying a used car. Was the machinery "tuned up" regularly? Have any parts been replaced recently? Pay special attention to parts that seem to have a tendency to wear out frequently. If a particular bearing or some other part has been replaced more than normal wear and tear would warrant, it could be that there's a larger problem. In other words, you may be getting a lemon. Also look to see if any parts might need to be replaced soon. You wouldn't want to buy a car that was going to need a new clutch in 1,000 miles—at least not at the price the owner is asking. It's basically the same thing with car wash equipment.

- *Water quality.* In Chapter 5, where we discussed testing your water for hardness, we mentioned that hard water tends to make equipment wear out a bit faster than if the water is soft. You might want to ask the current owner about the conditions the machinery was used under. Ask specifically what the level of water hardness (how many grains of hardness) was under typical operating conditions. If it was anything more than four, you may be buying a piece of equipment that will have a shorter than average service life.

- *Reasons the current owner is selling.* This should be an obvious question. You want to know why the current owner sees the need to get rid of used equipment. Did he just buy brand-new equipment as part of a major renovation or overhaul? Or does his new equipment look pretty much the same as what he's trying to sell you? If it's the latter, you might suspect there's some specific problem with this equipment. Is he going out of business? This is probably a good sign (for you, that is, not him). If the current owner is selling off his equipment because he no longer needs it, it's certainly a better sign than an owner who clearly could use the equipment but is trying to unload it.

Price vs. Reliability

Is there a correlation between price and reliability? Generally speaking, yes, but within reason. There is very expensive car wash equipment out there, and it's very good, reliable stuff. There's also some not-so-expensive equipment out there that's very good, reliable stuff. In other words, a higher price doesn't always mean it's the best for you. In general, the very expensive equipment is going to offer more in terms of special options and performance than cheaper systems. Both might hold up just as well; it's just that one may look a little snazzier or provide an extra little bit of "oomph" for your customers.

In practice, those extra options probably aren't going to add much to your bottom line. If anything, you may wind up losing customers because you have to charge a higher price to justify the more expensive price you paid for the equipment. The bottom line is that, as long as you go with a manufacturer that has a good track record of producing quality equipment, you shouldn't have a problem.

While we can't tell you exactly what type and brand of equipment to buy, we can tell you what you're going to need to get started. Let's take a look at the wash-related equipment you'll need for the type of car wash you plan to open.

Self-Service Equipment

A self-service car wash is going to be the easiest and least expensive wash to equip. There are any number of different combinations of equipment and services you can provide, which can make your start-up costs vary. But generally, you can expect to spend around $15,000 a bay to equip your wash.

So what will that $15,000 buy? The basic piece of equipment you're going to need is a power-wash unit that dispenses hot, soapy water for washing, and clean water for a rinse cycle. There are other options you can add, such as special cycles that can make your self-service what might be considered "high end." The options include a pre-soak, tire-cleaning, engine-cleaning, or wax-dispensing cycle—all options that your customers might find appealing.

To clean their cars, customers will put money or tokens into your machine, which will activate the cleaning "wand" (where all of this stuff comes out). This, of course, means you're going to need a bill changer on the premises to allow people to get the tokens they're going to need to activate the machinery. Plan on spending around $750 for each change machine.

You may be asking why what seems like an inexpensive setup costs so much. Well, because a self-service car wash is a lot like an iceberg—what the customer actually sees is really only a small part of all the equipment that makes it work. To start, the dispenser isn't just a hose with a brush attached to it; it's a sophisticated high-pressure, water-dispensing system. It also has the ability to mix soap with the water in very precise amounts to give the best cleaning capability. If you have an option that allows customers to apply wax, it has to have the ability to do that as well.

Unless you expect your water to heat itself, you're going to need a fairly substantial water heater. How large will depend on a whole bunch of factors, including the number of bays you have, how many customers you serve, and the style of your equipment. Your supplier will be able to recommend the correct size for your particular situation.

You're probably also going to need a system to soften your water (these run in the

Dollar Stretcher

Water reclamation systems don't only cut down on your water bill, they can also reduce your water-heating expenses by as much as 50 percent. Plus, they can reduce your soap usage by 35 to 50 percent, according to the folks at www.washguys.com.

Stat Fact

According to a recent report by the International Carwash Association, 86 percent of self-service owners say vacuums are the most popular extra service they offer. For conveyor washes, whether full-service or exterior-conveyor only, wax is the most popular add-on.

range of $4,000 to $5,000 for a basic system) and a "weep" system. A weep is something that allows for a continuous flow of water through your equipment and helps prevent frozen wands and pipes when the temperature dips below freezing. Wands either come equipped with a weep system or not, so be sure to ask your distributor before you buy.

Depending on your specific location, you may also need some sort of water-reclamation system. What these systems do is to essentially recycle the water so that you aren't dumping thousands of gallons of water into the sewer system. Even if you aren't required to have one, you may want to look into it anyway. These systems can save tremendous amounts of water by taking the soapy wash water, "reclaiming" it, and then using it again for the next washer. Basically, the only time exclusively fresh water is used when you operate with one of these systems is during the wash cycle. The cost of the system (approximately $15,000 for a basic system) may very well be offset by the money you'll save on your water bills.

You're also going to need some type of floor heater, unless of course you live somewhere where it never, ever gets below freezing. A floor heater will help get rid of ice that may accumulate on the floors of your bays during cold periods (cost range $3,000 to $5,000). People can't wash cars in the dark, so you're also going to need some sort of lighting system, especially if you plan on leaving your wash open at night or 24 hours a day (see the "Lighting" section on page 71).

In terms of your absolutely essential equipment, that's pretty much it. There are a whole host of other things you might want to invest in, and we'll get to those in a second. But first, we're going to give you some ideas about how to set up one of the most important sections of your car wash—the equipment room. This is where the rest of that iceberg resides. It's easy to ignore this and not put much thought into what it's going to look like. After all, it's the bays your customers will see, not the equipment room. Despite this, spend a little bit of time thinking about the layout of the room, since it's a lot easier (and cheaper) to get things done right the first time rather than having to

Bright Idea

Think about what extra bells and whistles you can provide that will make your car wash a more pleasant experience. One owner has a regular customer who routinely runs his car through his automatic bay two or three times in a single visit simply because he likes the color bubbles the soap creates! He says they relax him.

go back later and make changes. If you're buying an existing wash, you can still take the time now to change things around a bit if they aren't to your liking.

A number of owners think installing bathroom facilities in the equipment room is a good idea. Even if customers won't use it, you might like these facilities when you're spending hours on the premises cleaning your bays or doing some routine equipment maintenance. You also want to leave plenty of room for supplies, since this is really the only safe place you can store this stuff on the lot.

Your change machine is vitally important. In essence, this is your on-the-spot bank. Whatever money is in that change machine represents all the money you've made since the last time you emptied it. If you pick up your money once a day, and thieves steal a day's worth of revenue, that's 14 percent of your weekly revenue gone. Try to locate the machine in an area that's very visible. If you put it behind a wall or some other obstruction, thieves will have a much easier time breaking into it—and your customers will have a hard time finding it. You may also want to think about getting two change machines. The reason is that if one breaks down, you'll still have one

---

Automatically Speaking

If your new car wash business is going to be primarily a self-service operation, you still may want to consider installing an in-bay automatic unit as a supplement. There are some compelling reasons for doing this. The easiest one to argue is that a bay with an automatic rollover unit installed will often be more profitable than a self-service bay. An automatic could pull in 300 percent more revenue than a self-service bay alone. One owner we interviewed, Richard K., who has operated a self-service wash in the Chicago suburbs for 17 years, wishes he had more than the one in-bay automatic unit he has now. The reason? It makes him more money a unit than his bread-and-butter self-service bays.

Another compelling reason to consider adding an in-bay automatic unit is that you have the potential to significantly expand your customer base. As we've stated before, there are basically four types of car washers: the home washer, the do-it-yourself washer who patronizes self-service washes, the exterior-only washer who visits either exterior-conveyor washes or in-bay automatic washes, and the full-service customer. When you can combine two of these market segments, especially at the "low-rent" end of the spectrum, you've effectively captured about 50 percent of the car wash market. Customers who might normally have driven past your wash on their way to the exterior conveyor down the street, might reconsider if they can get an in-bay automatic wash from you—especially if it's more convenient for them or if it can provide a wash that's close in quality, but that will generally cost less.

in working order. If people can't get access to change or tokens to operate your wash, you might as well not even be open.

Now let's get to a couple of the other options we were talking about. Basically, these will consist of vacuuming facilities and vending machines. These may seem like small potatoes compared to the actual car washing service itself, but that's not really true. These offline services can dramatically boost your bottom line.

Let's talk about vending machines first. You can sell pretty much anything you can think of in these machines, from soft drinks and snacks to air fresheners and condoms. You may want to be a bit careful about the kinds of things you sell. As one owner puts it, "Don't sell anything in your machines you won't mind cleaning up off the floor." But you don't want to rule anything out simply because it's not your standard vending-machine fare.

Vacuum islands are another way to capture more revenue for each car. The number of vacuum islands you install is up to you, but you want to try to strike a balance between making sure that the facilities are easy for your customers to use (i.e., there aren't ten cars stacked up in line waiting for them to get free) and not having them sit idle. One island for every two bays might be a reasonable place to start, since you can always install more islands at a later date if you find that they're a popular option.

Another option you have is to create an entirely new type of bay—one that isn't self-service at all. This would be a bay that houses automatic washing equipment. Since this is really a distinct type of wash all its own, we'll devote an entire section to it next.

In-Bay Automatic Equipment

An in-bay automatic car wash is sort of a compromise between a self-service and an exterior-conveyor wash. This equipment is usually housed in a bay similar to one that you'd find at a self-service wash, except it's bigger. It's also more expensive to equip (about $30,000 to $40,000, or two to three times the cost of equipping a single self-service bay). Those are the downsides—larger space requirements and a bigger investment in terms of capital. It's also probably going to be a bit harder to maintain, since there are simply more moving, automated parts. Furthermore, installing an in-bay automatic unit really creates a domino effect throughout the rest of your facility. For example, you'll probably have to install a larger water heater and pump system to keep up with the demands of the automatic equipment. (Your distributor will be able to help you determine exactly what you need to do to have everything functioning properly.) This cost is in addition to the cost of the equipment. The upside is that you can generally expect more revenue from an in-bay automatic wash, and it's still a self-serve inasmuch as you may not need an attendant present all the time.

An in-bay automatic rollover unit will generally consist of a series of rollers that dispense soapy water and then provide a fresh water rinse. That's the basic setup. You can also opt for extras such as a wax cycle, an undercoating cycle and a wheel cleaner—all

Beware!

Think there's no need to post instructions around your equipment? One owner who was having trouble with his equipment opened the coin box to find a dollar bill folded up in the size of a quarter and stuffed through the slot. It's an amusing story, but if the owner hadn't discovered it right away, that bay would have been out of operation for hours.

of which will add to the price of the unit. However, these options can pay for themselves with the extra revenue they'll generate.

There is a note of caution about automatic rollover equipment. They have a bit of a "spotty" reputation (no pun intended) for their ability to do a thorough job of cleaning. Think of it this way: With a self-service wash, the customer is controlling how long the cycle is and can physically inspect the car before finishing up to make sure everything is clean. With an exterior conveyor, the equipment is more powerful, and there's usually someone to either prep the car for a better wash or to inspect it at the end of the cycle to make sure everything worked properly. With an in-bay automatic wash, you don't have any of these quality control safeguards.

Nevertheless, many self-service owners do opt to add at least one in-bay automatic unit as part of their package. They do this for a couple of reasons. First, it can help capture some of those customers who simply won't use self-service equipment. Second, as we said before, they can often generate more revenue than by having self-service bays alone. From what we've seen, if you want to go ahead and spend the extra money to install an in-bay automatic unit as part of an existing self-service wash, it's probably not a bad idea. But if you expect an in-bay automatic wash to be your sole source of revenue, you might want to think twice. Why? You'll see them at convenience stores or gas stations—in other words, places that aren't necessarily treating the car washing service as their main source of revenue. There might simply be too much competition in your area for an in-bay automatic wash only. You may be able to beat (or at least coexist) with your competition by offering self-service equipment and an in-bay automatic unit. Remember, self-service and in-bay automatic patrons are two different kinds of customers. But with an in-bay automatic wash alone, you may not be able to beat the gas station a couple blocks away with an automatic rollover wash that costs about half of what you charge—and offers the opportunity for customers to get gas at the same time.

Exterior-Conveyor and Full-Service Equipment

This is the big daddy of equipment start-up costs. Equipping a site with an exterior-conveyor tunnel can easily cost you in the range of $100,000 to $350,000. You can buy various tunnel sizes depending on the restrictions imposed by the size of your lot. The tunnels themselves will generally vary in length ranging from 70 feet to 100 feet. Most exterior-conveyor washes do basically the same thing—dispense soap, wash the car, rinse the car, apply wax or a rust-inhibiting undercoat, and dry the car—though there are variations. Hanna-Sherman, a major equipment manufacturer in Portland, Oregon, constructs its tunnels in an open design, which it says is based on research that shows that customers generally aren't comfortable with the closed-in feeling you get when you ride through some conveyor tunnels.

When you start researching the type of equipment you're going to buy, try to look at it through the eyes of your customers. What kind of washing experience would you like to have if you were visiting your wash? This can help you decide between two otherwise equal distributors or manufacturers.

The difference between a full-service and exterior-conveyor really has very little to do with equipment, but rather with the extra services the owner provides, i.e., vacuuming, glass cleaning, interior cleaning, etc. If you're planning on providing a full-service wash, you can decide whether or not to install vacuuming stations on your lot. It's probably a good idea to do so if you plan to offer an exterior-only cleaning package so that you can allow your customers to do the interior part themselves. If you're going to be exclusively an exterior wash, then vacuum services are going to be almost essential. Plan on spending about $1,000 for each vacuum unit.

Of course, you'll also need the other standard equipment that we discussed for self-service and in-bay automatic washes, such as a water heater, water softener system, and water reclamation system, though these may cost you more for a conveyor wash. A water heater may run you $2,000 to $4,000, a water softening system may cost you around $6,000, and a water reclamation system will be close to $25,000. You'll also need one or more automatic dryers, at a cost of $15,000 a unit.

Retail/Lot Equipment

If you're buying an existing car wash, there probably isn't that much that you can do about the existing infrastructure of the business (i.e., building size and construction, machinery and equipment placement, etc.). However, there are other areas that you can change, including landscaping, lighting, signage, and similar items. If you're building from scratch, of course, everything is in your power to decide—within the confines of your space and budget. So either way, you do have some items to consider in designing the look and functionality of your business.

To Shade or Not to Shade

If you're providing customers with facilities to vacuum or detail their own cars after they've gone through your wash, one of the decisions you're going to have to make is whether to provide shade for your customers. This isn't just a question of being a nice guy and wanting your customers to be comfortable. It's a matter of dollars and cents. Customers probably aren't going to want to use your vacuums if they have to stand in the hot sun on a scorching day to do it. On the other side of the coin, if it's frigid, they might welcome the sun's warmth. What should you do? First of all, consider your weather. If you're located in a hot climate, some sort of shade or roof can be a great idea. If you're in a more moderate climate that has both hot and cold times of the year, what about some sort of retractable shade system? The cost for an area that can accommodate three cars at once (about 18 by 27 feet) is around $3,500. See the Appendix for vendor contact information.

Security

Security is a major concern for today's car wash owners. We're not saying there's a nationwide crime spree occurring at our country's car washes, but there have been several high profile cases of major crimes, such as murder, being committed against car wash customers. These kinds of incidents are unfortunate for an industry already struggling with a bad reputation in many people's minds. It's easy to see why getting a reputation for being unsafe will severely cripple your new wash. For this reason, you should give some serious consideration to how you'll make your wash as safe as you can for your customers. You're also going to need to concentrate on how to make your wash as safe as you can for you and your employees. Let's focus on some steps you can take to increase safety on your premises.

A good security system will accomplish three things: It will safeguard your customers, it will safeguard you and your employees, and it will safeguard your money. Exactly what kind of system you install is going to be dependent on a number of factors. You can ask the previous owner what worked for him if you're buying an existing wash, or the architect or supplier if you're building a wash from scratch. Price

---

Covering Up

If you own a self-service car wash, it probably won't be too long before you start searching for the best way to cover the walls of your wash bays. Here's a tip: Some owners say fiberglass wallboards are the way to go. They're more attractive than exposed brick and are easier to clean, too. One thing you're probably going to want to avoid is paint. For one thing, the kind of paint you'll have to buy is very expensive. Plus, it tends to deteriorate after only a year or two, meaning you're either going to have to repaint frequently or put up with a wash that looks run-down.

All about Garbage

Some owners have problems with trash cans blowing over in strong winds or having them kicked over by vandals. Want a simple solution? Try contacting a local concrete company to help you out with a concrete receptacle that's similar to what you see on some city streets and outside fast-food restaurants. Because they're extremely heavy, there's very little chance anyone will be able to tip them over, or worse yet, steal them.

should be a factor in your decision, but remember, just one crime at your car wash can cost you lots of money in lost goods and lost customers. A simple security camera might cost only several hundred dollars, while an elaborate networked system could run you several thousand dollars. The cheapest alternative, one that should cost less than $100, would be to buy fake security cameras and position them at highly visible points around your wash. Sometimes just the threat of being taped might be enough to deter crime.

Lighting

There's more to creating a safe environment than just installing the latest high-tech equipment to deter criminals. It should also be your goal to create the perception in people's minds that they'll be safe pulling into your wash, getting out of their cars, and using your services. You can accomplish this in several ways.

How and where you choose to install exterior lights is an important consideration, especially for unmanned car washes, such as self-service washes that are operational 24 hours a day. You need adequate lighting in the bays themselves, as well as in the surrounding lot areas. You don't want your bays to be an oasis of light while the rest of your property remains a desert of darkness. Exactly what you'll be able to do in terms of outdoor lighting may be limited by local ordinances. On the flip side, local laws or regulations may require extensive lighting. Whichever side of the coin your municipality falls on, it's always safer to err on the side of caution—if you're unsure as to whether you need extra lighting somewhere on your lot, it's probably best to go ahead and install something.

In the bays themselves you're going to want to strike a balance between providing enough adequate lighting that will allow your customers to feel safe and do a good job washing their cars, while not blinding them with light so bright that it becomes uncomfortable. This may sound like a trivial matter, but you'd be surprised at the debate many self-service owners have about what wattage and type of bulbs to use in their bays. There doesn't seem to be one solution that works for everyone, but bulbs that are 250 watts are a pretty common choice, so you might want to start there and make adjustments if need be. Lighting may cost you anywhere from $500 to $1,500, depending on the size of your car wash.

Signage

There's a quite lengthy discussion of signage in the marketing chapter (Chapter 10), so we'll only touch on this subject briefly here. Your exterior signs should be as big as you can possibly make them. People need to see your sign before they think about stopping at your business, and they also need to know at a glance what you're offering. For that reason, the words "car wash" must be the most prominent thing potential customers see.

Interior signage should serve to explain procedures if you have areas of your wash that are left unattended, such as self-serve bays, automatic bays, or vacuum islands. They should also make it easy for a customer to reach someone if there's a problem and clearly explain the pricing system and what the customers will get for their money.

If you need to construct a sign from scratch, it can get pretty expensive—anywhere from $5,000 to $10,000 for both a sign with your business name and something that holds your menu board. Interior signage is much more reasonable and should only run you a few hundred dollars.

> **Tip...**
>
> **Smart Tip**
>
> For your interior signage, especially in self-service bays, use pictures and graphics in addition to words to explain how to use the equipment. Not everyone who washes their car can read English, and you certainly don't want to lose customers simply because they speak a different language.

Landscaping

Without overstating its importance, landscaping is a fairly essential part of most car washes. With that said, you should realize that a beautifully landscaped lot is no substitute for a competitive price and superior service. In fact, some new owners get into trouble by thinking that they'll be able to charge well above the average price in their area simply because their wash is the most attractive. While that's not true, what is true is that proper landscaping can certainly make a difference in the way your wash is perceived in customers' eyes.

You don't have to go overboard and hire professional gardeners to outfit your lot with lots of expensive shrubbery, but give some thought to designing something that is both practical (i.e., easy to maintain and doesn't interfere with the wash process) and visually appealing. If you do this yourself, you should be able to get it done for around $200 for a small lot, to maybe $500 for a larger parcel.

Employees

Although we go into much greater detail about employees in Chapter 8, we're mentioning the topic here because you're going to want to give some thought to the role your employees will play in the overall setup of your wash. How many will you need and for what shifts? Will you hire full- or part-time employees?

Most owners pay their workers a few dollars above the federal minimum wage. According to a recent survey by *Professional Carwashing & Detailing*, a typical starting wage was $6.46 an hour, which is just about in line with what the entrepreneurs we interviewed are paying. Generally, this rate will be higher in larger cities or places with lots of competition for the same labor pool, and lower in rural areas or in places where the supply of workers outstrips the demand. In addition, some of your employees will need to be paid at higher rates depending on the functions they perform (see Chapter 8).

Financing Your New Wash

Most new car wash owners are going to need some type of financing to get started. In Chapter 9, there's a fairly detailed discussion of rate of return, or return on investment (ROI). This is one of the main areas where that number is going to come into play and here's why: Borrowing money to finance a new business makes sense if you can expect to earn more of a return to repay that loan. In other words, if you obtain a loan at 9 percent interest, you had better hope to make more than a 9 percent rate of return from your car wash. Otherwise, what's the point? How much more is somewhat a matter of opinion, but certainly you're going to want to make enough to justify the risks of investing in the somewhat risky proposition of a car wash, as opposed to the safer investment of a treasury bill or bank certificate of deposit.

▲

Start-Up Costs for Conveyor Washes

Listed below are hypothetical start-up costs for two conveyor washes. The first is for a full-service car wash, built as a new business. The second is for an exterior-conveyor car wash, bought as an existing business. Compare these start-up costs to get an idea of what your own start-up costs may look like.

Start-Up Costs	Full-Service	Exterior-Conveyor
Cost of existing business	$0	$1,000,000
Building costs (including tunnel, equipment room, waiting room, and office space)	200,000	0
Land (one-month lease)	6,250 (25,000 sq. ft.)	0
Wash-related equipment (including power-wash units, vacuums, automatic dryers, water heater, water reclamation, water softener)	284,000	0
Retail/lot equipment (including shaded vacuum area, vending machines, change machines, signage, security system, trash receptacles, bathroom fixtures, cash register, lighting, inventory)	37,250	0
Office equipment and supplies (furniture, computer and software, printer, phone, fax, shredder, calculator, paper, and miscellaneous supplies)	8,050	2,000
Employee wages (for one month)	28,000 (17 full-time and 13 part-time employees)	8,000 (4 full-time and 5 part-time employees)
Cleaning supplies	1,900	1,200
Waxes and other protectants	700	350

Start-Up Costs for Conveyor Washes, continued

Start-Up Costs	Full-Service	Exterior-Conveyor
Other washing supplies (rags, fragrance, etc.)	$700	$350
Retail supplies (gift items, refreshments, auto accessories)	750	100
Grand opening advertising	1,000	1,000
Legal fees	1,000	750
Annual insurance premium	2,000	1,000
Utility hookups	5,500	5,500
Licenses and permits (including vending and business licenses)	1,000	1,000
Environmental studies and testing	2,000	2,000
Appraisal costs	1,000	1,000
Market analysis and research (demographic and feasibility studies, consultant fee, etc.)	5,000	5,000
Professional memberships	450	450
Total Start-Up Costs	**$586,550**	**$1,029,700**

Start-Up Costs for Self-Serve Washes

Take a look at these start-up costs for two self-serve car washes. One scenario is for building a combination self-service and in-bay automatic car wash. The other is for buying an existing self-service car wash with two wash bays.

Start-Up Costs	3 Self-Service Bays and 1 In-Bay Automatic Unit	2 Self-Service Bays Only
Cost of existing business	$0	$125,000
Building costs	80,000 ($20,000 a bay)	0
Land (one-month lease)	1,000 (10,000 sq. ft.)	0
Wash-related equipment (including power-wash units, vacuums, water heater, water reclamation, water softener)	99,750	0
Retail/lot equipment (including shaded vacuum area, vending machines, change machines, signage, security system, trash receptacles, lighting, inventory)	3,000	0
Office equipment and supplies (furniture, computer and software, printer, phone, fax, shredder, calculator, paper, and miscellaneous supplies)	2,615	1,000
Employee wages (for one month)	1,250 (1 part time)	0 (no employees)
Cleaning supplies	600	275
Waxes and other protectants	100	50
Other washing supplies (rags, fragrance, etc.)	150	75
Retail supplies for vending machines	300	200

Start-Up Costs for Self-Serve Washes, continued

Start-Up Costs	3 Self-Service Bays and 1 In-Bay Automatic Unit	2 Self-Service Bays Only
Grand opening advertising	$500	$250
Legal fees	500	500
Annual insurance premium	1,500	800
Utility hookups	5,500	5,500
Licenses and permits (including vending and business licenses)	1,000	1,000
Environmental studies and testing	2,000	2,000
Appraisal costs	750	500
Market analysis and research (demographic and feasibility studies, consultant fee, etc.)	5,000	5,000
Professional memberships	450	450
Total Start-Up Costs	**$205,965**	**$142,600**

Inventory
and Pricing

O ne of the nice things about a car wash, and one of the things that attracts people to the business, is the fact that it's possible to run the business with hardly any inventory other than the supplies you need to clean cars. With that said, you may well elect to have some type of inventory beyond that—things such as air fresheners, snacks, and cleaning equipment that your customers can purchase either in a gift shop or from a vending machine.

We've already mentioned the importance of maintaining a full supply of the materials you'll need to avoid running short during peak washing periods. Whatever method you devise to keep track of your inventory, the goal is always the same: To have on hand those supplies that you'll need to keep your business running smoothly and offer customers a wide selection.

In some ways there's an art to managing inventory, though most accountants would tell you they have it pretty much down to a science. As a car wash owner, nobody will know better than you what your customers want and in what quantity. Having only the bare minimum on hand or ignoring the importance of certain premium items hurts your ability to up-sell those customers for whom a clean, well-maintained car is a sense of pride.

On the other hand, there is also such a thing as overstocking. While it may seem safer to have too much than too little, it's smarter to have just enough. In this chapter, we'll get into the various methods for determining what's "just enough," and we'll look at the basic supplies you're going to need.

Basic Supplies for Your Car Wash

Water isn't something you inventory, neither is air if you offer vacuum services. So what will your inventory consist of? Basically, you need to think about car wash materials, offline car-care items, and offline items not related to car care. Depending on what type of car wash you open, you may only need some of these types of inventory items. For example, if you offer the bare-bones minimum, such as a couple of self-service bays and a few vacuum stations, the only inventory you have to worry about falls under car wash materials.

- *Car wash materials.* This category will encompass everything you use to perform your service, from soap to wax. Depending on the type of wash you have, it might also include things such as undercarriage rust inhibitors or fragrance. Anything that gets used up in the process of washing cars goes here.

- *Offline car-care items.* These are the things you can sell that help customers clean cars themselves, but that aren't part of your wash process. Products in vending machines like air fresheners, towels, or Armor All would fall into this category.

- *Offline items not related to car care.* This would be everything from snack foods to soft drinks that you might sell in a vending machine to things such as magazines, fuzzy dice, or other odds and ends that you might sell in a gift shop.

Simple Ways to Keep Track of Inventory

To keep an eye on your inventory, you're going to need some sort of logbook or computer software that allows you to track what you've bought, what you've sold, and what you have on hand. You can probably use any one of a number of standard business software packages or get one geared specifically toward car washes. WashRemote, a product from Imagine Software Solutions in Corona, California, is one you may want to check out (see the Appendix for contact information). This will help you keep an adequate supply of material on hand without having a lot of extra stuff lying around.

If you're buying an existing wash, you can ask the previous owner how much of each product he ordered and how often. Then you can modify his schedule over time if you notice it's not the best way to do it.

If you're starting fresh, go back to your business plan and determine how many cars you expect to wash in any given month. Then talk to your distributor or manufacturer to find out, based on that number, how much of the various supplies you're going to need. Again, if you find over time that you're consistently overestimating or underestimating what you need, make the necessary changes as you go.

Retail Items

It might be best, especially as someone who is new to the business, to start small at first if you plan to offer items not directly related to car washing. To see how you can manage your inventory of these items effectively, let's take air fresheners as an example. These are pretty popular with many car wash customers. Let's say you buy 100 air fresheners for $25 and initially price them at $1 each. In the first week you offer them, you sell five. That means, on those five items, you made a total profit of $3.75. (Each product cost you $.25; you sold them for a buck, netting you $.75; $.75 x 5 items = $3.75.)

In the second week, you sell five more. Now you're beginning to realize that they may not move quickly enough at $1, and they're taking up display space from another item that's selling very well—a change holder for the dashboard, for example. This is when inventory becomes a concern, and also the point where inventory and pricing collide. You've got to move those air fresheners to make room for the change holders, so you drop the price of the air fresheners to $.50.

Finally, people start to buy them and you can use the free space to display more change holders. What has this taught you? In the future, you're going to want to order fewer air fresheners and more change holders. That's a very basic way to control inventory, but it's essentially what it's all about. You want to order enough of each item to sell it at the markup that you want.

▲

Decisions, Decisions

When you start making inventory decisions, one of the first questions you'll probably face is what to offer besides your basic wash services. Do you want to offer auto supplies (air fresheners, cleaning products, etc.), refreshments, food, or some other products you think would be helpful to your customers?

One thing you want to keep in mind when making this decision is your profit margin on each item. In some ways, this may turn out to be even more important than demand. Soft drinks may sell well, and it may seem like a great deal if a large supplier is willing to give you the vending machine for free. However, after you account for stocking the machine and paying for the electricity to run it, you may wind up making next to nothing in profit.

The best products to offer are those that cost next to nothing, but that have a high perceived value for your customers. Typical fare such as soft drinks and candy bars may not be the best choice. Talk to your customers and find out what they'd like to see you offer—they can often be your best source for market research.

By logging and tracking what you order, what you sell, and how much profit you make from each item, you'll start to see patterns. You'll start to realize that you could use some more change holders and fewer air fresheners, or vice versa as the case may be.

Pricing Offline Items

Take a look at what others are charging for the items you're offering. If the convenience store across the street is selling a Coke for $.75, you probably aren't going to be able to sell it for $1.50. You may have some flexibility here—since you have a somewhat captive audience—but in general, the prices for these types of goods should just about match what others are charging.

If it turns out that, for whatever reason, you're able to make a much larger profit selling candy bars than Coke, you may want to drop the soft drinks and instead devote that space to selling more candy bars.

Pricing Your Services

The type of car wash you run will determine how you price your services in this respect. If you run a self-service wash, you're going to charge for the time the customer

Stat Fact

According to *Professional Carwashing & Detailing* magazine, the average price for each minute charged by self-service washes is slightly more than $.32.

uses the equipment. If you operate an in-bay automatic, a full-service, or an exterior-conveyor wash, you're going to charge for each wash, no matter how long it takes.

Pricing at a Self-Service Wash

The first thing you want to determine is the start-up cost for the customer. In other words, how much money does he have to put into your machine just to turn it on? Generally, this is going to be around $1, give or take $.25 or so. A common cycle length for that first dollar is around four minutes. After the first cycle, you can charge the same amount for each additional four minutes, or raise or lower the price. For example, you could go with $1.25 for the first four minutes and a quarter a minute after that. Vacuum services are generally priced in the same way.

How much you actually charge will depend on:

- *Your facilities.* The better maintained and newer they are, the more you can charge.
- *Your location.* The more affluent your customers are, the more you can charge.
- *Your competition.* The less competition you have, the more you can charge.

What should also factor into your decision is the amount of profit you need to meet your projections. You don't want to set your prices at a point where you're not making any money, but you also don't want to price yourself out of the market.

A good rule of thumb is to visit other self-service washes in your area. Find out what they're charging, and then match or beat them. If you truly have superior facilities and a far better location, you might be able to get away with charging a bit more than your competitors, but don't bank on it.

Another way to think about pricing is to figure out how much each wash cycle costs you to provide, and then what percentage above that you can add as your profit. For example, say it costs you $.65 a wash cycle in cleaning supplies, utilities, and other overhead costs. If you charge the customer $1 a cycle, you'll net $.35 a cycle—that's roughly a 54 percent markup.

Pricing at an In-Bay Automatic Wash

Much the same strategy applies here, except you won't be charging by time, but rather by wash. Let's say you're going to charge $4 a wash, which is right around the industry average. This number should roughly be in line with what's being charged at other in-bay automatics in your area.

Stat Fact
The average price of a bestselling, full-service package at a typical full-service car wash is nearly $18, says *Professional Carwashing & Detailing* magazine.

To look at it another way, let's say you want a 50 percent markup over what it costs you to provide the car wash. If it costs you $2 a wash, you want to charge at least $3. If this is your situation and you can still get away with charging $4, then so be it. But you need to be aware of your bottom line to make sure that you're paying yourself enough money.

Pricing at a Conveyor Wash

This is essentially the same as pricing an in-bay automatic wash, except the numbers go up. On average, the price for an exterior-conveyor wash is a little more than $5. For a full-service wash, the average price is close to $9.

Using your desired markup, and taking into account the prices of your competitors, you'll be able to determine if you want to price above or below these figures. It might cost you around $4.50 to give a car the full-service treatment, so a price of $9 is a 100 percent markup. If it costs you $2.50 for an exterior-conveyor wash, the markup is 100 percent if you're charging $5 a wash.

Your Menu of Services

Deciding what services to offer is one part of the equation. Deciding how to offer them is the other. You have a couple of choices here. One choice is to list the basic price of a car wash, and then list each add-on separately along with its price. This isn't the best idea. It's better to package your services. The more decisions you force your customers to make, the less likely it is that they'll choose what you want them to choose. For example, which is easier for your customer to say: "I'll take a wash and presoak and tire cleaning and wax and spot-free rinse and undercarriage protection and rust inhibitor," or "I'll take the deluxe package"? Get the point?

What's the best way to construct your menu of services? It should give a good indication of exactly what the customer is paying for. Granted, you probably won't be able to put everything on that sign. That's part of the reason your service writer is there—to describe the various levels of service and, to explain why the customer would be happier upgrading to one of your premium packages.

Stat Fact
According to a recent study by the International Carwash Association, price is the number-one reason most home washers choose to forego visits to a professional wash facility.

Stat Fact

According to the International Carwash Association, 58 percent of full-service car wash owners who plan to add a profit center to their existing wash say they plan to start selling gasoline. That's more than five times the next most popular add-on, a convenience store.

Nonetheless, you want your customers to have some idea of what they want before your service writer gets to them.

Your menu of services should also serve as a sales tool. How you accomplish this is a bit more of an art than a science. In other words, it's easy to determine how big to make your lettering so that most drivers can easily read it. But it's a bit trickier to determine exactly what is going to make them choose a premium wash over a standard. It's probably not a bad idea to place your most expensive package at the top of the list. Some owners claim that customers often won't even read down the menu; they'll simply take the first package they see—which just turns out to be the most expensive package. Even if this is not the case, arranging your packages in order of most expensive to least expensive (rather than having no logical order) will make your menu of services easier for customers to deal with.

You can get creative with the names you attach to your packages as well. There's no reason you have to stick with the old stand-bys like "Basic Package" or "Deluxe Wash." Instead, why not try and incorporate some type of theme into your names. For example, one car wash owner who's located in a town with a large military population named one package the "Ship Shape Super Wash." Another owner who's located in a historic mining town tried "The 49er Protectant Plus," "Gold Miner Deluxe," and "Gold Pan Basic." Yet another owner, located near a space center in Texas, named his wash packages after various lunar missions—Mercury, Gemini, Apollo, etc. His deluxe package is called "Ultimate Splashdown." This can work especially well if the names of your wash packages are somehow tied into the name of your car wash itself. Not only does it make things more interesting for customers, but it can also help the name of your wash stick in their minds. Give it some thought. We're sure you'll come up with something just as creative.

There are some other techniques you can try to draw attention to your higher-priced packages. For instance, it's a proven fact in the advertising field that the word "free" is by far the most effective at attracting the attention of customers. You might try using this as part of your signage. Let's say, for example, that after researching the competition and running through your own numbers, you decide to set the price for a deluxe wash package at $10. Let's also assume that this package includes the basic exterior wash, plus rust inhibitor, special wheel cleaning, wax, hand drying, and an interior vacuum. Those are the services you're going to provide for ten bucks no matter how you shake it. So why not call the interior vacuuming a free bonus? Or the wax, or the wheel cleaner, or whatever? Now, instead of your menu simply reading something like:

> *Deluxe Wash: Full exterior wash, wheel brightener, wax, rust inhibitor,*
> *hand dry, and interior vacuuming, $10.*

Now it reads:

> *Deluxe Wash: Full exterior wash, wheel brightener, wax, rust inhibitor,*
> *hand dry, PLUS FREE INTERIOR VACUUMING, $10.*

Which approach is more effective? Which is more likely to give the consumers the feeling that they've truly gotten their money's worth? You can guess.

Now that you've had your fill of inventory and pricing issues, we're going to turn to another topic essential to running a successful car wash. In the next chapter, we'll tackle all the major issues that come with hiring employees for your car wash.

Car Wash
Employees

Probably the only type of car wash business that won't require you to hire employees is a self-service car wash. And even then, there will be times when you need to have someone on the premises.

Most evidence suggests that having an attendant on duty will increase the revenue you derive from any in-bay automatics you may have installed. The duties of a self-service/in-bay automatic wash employee are not nearly as extensive as those for an exterior-conveyor or full-service wash. You might want to think of these employees as caretakers. They are available to help customers should a problem arise, answer questions about the proper way to use equipment, make change, and generally watch over the operation to make sure everything runs smoothly.

According to a recent report by the International Carwash Association (ICA), the average self-service/in-bay automatic wash used some combination of one or two part- and full-time workers to handle these tasks. In terms of what you can expect to pay for these employees, plan to spend anywhere from $16,000 a year on the high end (according to the ICA report) to around $10,000 a year on the low end (according to a recent survey by *Professional Carwashing & Detailing* magazine). This amounts to anywhere from 10 to 20 percent of your gross sales. Of course, you may want to handle these responsibilities yourself rather than hiring someone to do it for you.

For exterior-only or full-service washes, you're going to need employees. The exact positions you'll need to fill will vary depending on the services you offer, but in general you can expect to need service writers (also called greeters), cashiers, technicians, and send-off workers. Certain full-service washes may also need employees to vacuum and perform other interior work. Although you may think that a process as automated as a car wash would require very little money for employees, industry statistics reveal that the truth is very different. You can expect your labor costs to be about 20 percent of total revenues for an exterior-only wash, and close to 40 percent for a full-service wash. That's quite a chunk. To understand why the costs are so high, it's important to know what these employees do, and how each contributes to your business.

Service Writers/Greeters

These are the revenue-generating employees . . . if they're good. A service writer is the person who greets customers as they pull into your wash and takes their order. That sounds simple enough, and it pretty much is, but a good service writer will do more than just that. One of the keys to success in the car wash business is building your traffic count. Another key is what you do with that traffic count—i.e., how

Smart Tip

Think about where you will position your greeters or service-writers so that they can be the most visible for your customers. On busy days, they're going to be moving amongst the cars as they queue up outside the wash facility, but on slower days you should have some idea as to where you'd like them to be so that they can respond quickly when a customer pulls in.

well you maximize your per-car revenue. Good service writers will help you do that.

You want your service writers to have both the freedom and the incentive to up-sell your customers, not in a harsh or aggressive way, but in a way that demonstrates to the customer that the service writer knows what he's talking about and can make honest recommendations about what type of service is best for the customer's car. Mike G., a car wash owner in Carson, California, kept the existing service writers on when he bought his car wash six years ago. He could have brought in his own people and probably paid them a bit less, but he decided it wasn't worth it. Why? Simply because they knew what they were doing. They knew the regular customers, and they were good. They're still working for him today and make decent money doing it because they're successful up-sellers. How can you encourage your service writers to up-sell? Some type of incentive program is going to be required. We'll return to this topic later in the chapter.

Service writers need to have outstanding people skills. They need to be communicators. Appearance also counts, as does a true desire to meet customers and give them the best service you can. You should be able to easily spot those traits during the job interview. Does the applicant smile? Is he or she pleasant? Does he or she speak well? Is the applicant intelligent enough to learn the business and how the wash process works? This doesn't require a rocket scientist, but it's not a job for a grammar

Payment Pointers

What will employee wages look like for the various positions you'll need to fill? Keep this comparison in mind as a general guideline.

Service writers: $$$$$
(most will derive compensation from commissions on sales)

Cashiers: $$$

Technicians: $$

Send-off employees: $

school dropout either. Finally, can he or she take what they know about the wash and explain it to customers? If the applicant meets all those requirements, you've probably got a well-qualified candidate on your hands.

Cashiers

You know what cashiers do, so let's not waste space running through their basic duties in much detail. Above and beyond the standard duties, however, are some basic things your cashiers can do to increase your average sale for each car. Think about the last time you went in to a fast-food restaurant and tried to order something without fries. For just about anything you order (except maybe a hot fudge sundae), cashiers will ask almost without fail "Do you want fries with that?" Your cashiers could be doing the same type of thing. Not with fries, of course, but with gift certificates, wash booklets, air fresheners, or whatever.

It's a very simple matter to train your cashiers to up-sell. Simply make them aware of the products you have that your customers might be interested in. For instance, around the holidays, you might try a big push for gift certificates or coupon books that the customer can give away as gifts. Something as simple as "We're now offering a book of coupons good for ten washes at a discount. They make great stocking stuffers," can have a dramatic effect.

Your cashiers are also going to be one of the last people your customer sees before they leave your wash. Therefore, they're in a unique position to gather information. Teach them how to do this, and what you want to know to help you make your business the best it can be. For example, training your cashiers to ask the simple question "Were you satisfied with our service?" speaks volumes to your customers. You hope that your customers will all respond with a resounding "Yes." But what if they don't? What if one of them feels their car isn't as clean as they would have hoped. Therein lies the real value of having a good cashier. They can help fix the problem. If something went wrong mechanically, it may have resulted in a car being washed improperly. In this instance, a good cashier will be able to solve the problem by contacting a manager or other service technician to alert that person to the situation.

If there's some other reason the customer isn't satisfied—maybe the process took too long, another employee was rude or insulting, or he or she simply doesn't feel it was worth the money—you can set guidelines for how your cashiers should deal with these types of problems.

Bright Idea

Don't leave anything to chance with your attendants. Instead of just telling them what to do, create a checklist that they can follow each and every day. Include everything they should be doing throughout the day, from sweeping the lot to inspecting hoses and equipment. This helps ensure that nothing gets overlooked.

Sometimes, the remedy will be to contact you or the manager on duty to address the complaint. Other times, it may be to offer an apology and explain that the customer experienced a unique situation; that it doesn't usually take 45 minutes for a wash, but that today you were surprised by the unexpected volume. Just a few simple words of understanding can go a long way toward turning a dissatisfied customer into one who gives you at least a second chance.

In terms of the qualities that your cashiers should have, they're pretty much the same as those you need to look for in a service writer. You want pleasant employees who can interact with customers and make them feel welcome. Nobody wants to hand over money to a grumpy cashier. You also need to be able to trust them implicitly. After all, they're handling your money. Make sure to ask for references from previous employers and then call them. You'd be surprised how many business owners insist on obtaining references from job candidates but never do anything with the information.

Technicians

We're using this term as a catchall phrase to describe everybody else who works for you, except for your send-off employees (we'll discuss those next). These employees will be the ones doing the little extras that help your equipment do its job better. For instance, you might have a few employees applying presoak to the wheels, or even to the entire car. You may have another whose job it is to make sure the car is going through the wash in such a way that the chance for damage is minimized—someone whose job it is to remove detachable radio antennas and remind drivers to keep all windows closed, for example.

Your technicians also need to be customer-friendly, but don't need the refined people skills of employees who regularly interact with the customers, such as cashiers and service writers. Perhaps the most important quality technicians should possess is reliability. Having employees who you know are going to show up on time and do what is expected of them is important in any business. It is perhaps even more important in a business like car washing that requires shift work. Imagine a nurse who shows up late to work every day or a waiter who is consistently late for lunch service. It's the same thing with your car wash. If your presoak guy is an hour late for work, that's an hour that each and every customer who goes through your wash doesn't get the kind of quality service you want to provide.

Send-Off Employees

These are the employees who basically take care of anything that wasn't taken care of by your service writers, technicians, or other production workers. Depending on the services you offer and what the customer has purchased, these might include employees whose responsibility it is to towel dry the car when it emerges from the tunnel, vacuum the interior, clean and polish the rims and wheels, or dust and apply protectant to the interior.

The qualities you're looking for in your send-off employees are basically the same as those that you're looking for in your technicians or production workers. It's probably a good idea to train all your send-off employees to handle all the duties they might be assigned. In other words, don't just train them to vacuum the interior of cars; teach them the proper way to clean the windows and dry the cars, too. This will give you some scheduling options that wouldn't be available if you only had employees who knew only one small part of the overall process.

These will probably be the lowest paid of all your workers, and it's probably where you're going to see the most turnover. There's not a lot you can do about it, except for some of the ways we discuss below to keep your employee turnover below average. For this reason, you're going to need a sort of ongoing training program. One of the things you may want to consider doing in this area is to hire someone who is essentially going to serve as your department manager. He'll essentially be your sergeant for the rest of the send-off platoon. It will be his job to train and monitor the send-off employees. In exchange for the added responsibility, you can pay him a bit more and give him a few more perks.

Depending on how much control you want to give up, you could also allow him to make his own scheduling decisions for the send-off area, freeing you up to work on marketing strategies or other ways to grow the business. He might also be the one conducting the initial interviews when you make new hires for his area.

Where Can You Find Employees?

Now that you know what you should expect from each of your employees, we should probably talk a little bit about how to go about finding, hiring, and retaining the kind of quality people you need to make your car wash work.

College Students

You certainly aren't going to be making many trips to the college recruiting office to set up interviews with MBA graduates (unless you're looking for someone to take over full management responsibilities for your wash). However, you may be making trips to the local college to recruit the kind of part-time employees who make your wash function on a daily basis.

College students can be a great source of labor for a car wash. For one thing, they're willing to work for less money than someone with a family to support. For another, their schedules are often much more flexible than most people's. The only drawback is that these flexible schedules can make your scheduling procedure a bit more complicated than if you had a pool of employees available whenever you needed them to work. If you have many college students on your payroll, you're going to have to work around their class schedules, and just about everyone's is going to be different. And what about holidays? Stock your payroll exclusively with out-of-state college kids, and you may find yourself without any available workers over the Thanksgiving and Christmas holidays—not to mention spring break and summer vacation.

Retirees

At the other end of the spectrum are retirees. In fact, for many people, the label retiree simply doesn't apply. These are people who simply can't fathom the thought of spending their golden years fishing or simply relaxing. They want to work. In some ways, retirees may be even more desirable employees than college students. As a group, retirees may be more reliable. They may also be a bit more consistent, remaining available for work regardless of the time of year. Finally, because their income is most likely going to be supplemented by retirement plans or Social Security, they may be willing to accept jobs that pay a bit less.

Just as with hiring exclusively out-of-state college students, there is a drawback to hiring only retirees. For one thing, their physical stamina may not match up to some of your younger crewmembers. This isn't always going to be the case, but you can generally assume that a 19-year-old is going to be able to handle more physically demanding labor than a 70-year-old. You might also run into a situation where retirees miss more work due to illnesses.

Recent Immigrants

Immigrants, both young and old, also make up a sizeable portion of the car wash work force. There may be any number of reasons for this, but certainly one of them is that a car wash job provides an entry into the work force, with relatively few specialized skill requirements.

The drawbacks? Well, one of them could be the language barrier. You would hope that

> **Smart Tip** — *Tip...*
>
> Having trouble finding employees? One owner has found trailer parks to be a good source of employees. Try approaching the manager and asking if anyone in the complex is looking for work.

anyone you hire has at least a working command of the English language, if for no other reason than to allow you to train them. You can alleviate this problem by learning a common foreign language yourself or hiring managers or other employees who are bilingual and who can help you communicate.

Other Sources of Labor

If you expect to have any kind of life at all outside of your car wash, you're eventually going to have to hire someone who can function as an assistant manager to hold down the fort when you're not there. Running a car wash certainly isn't rocket science, but it isn't flipping burgers either. You may get lucky and find a student who, after working with you for a while, decides he'd like to make a career out of it. In such a case, maybe you can start training that employee on the finer points of running the business, grooming him so that one day you'll feel comfortable giving him the keys to the store, so to speak.

If not, you're going to have to find that type of employee somewhere else. Ideally, you'd be looking for someone with some managerial and business experience. It would be nice if that person was a college graduate, but it probably isn't required if he or she has some experience in the business or professional world.

The old method of taking out a want ad in the local paper certainly couldn't hurt. Perhaps a family member wants to get into the business or you have friends who know someone responsible who would be interested. Local high schools and community colleges might be another place to look. It's highly unlikely that you're going to turn over control of your business to a 17-year-old kid, but after you spend some time training him and start to get a feel for whether or not he's trustworthy and as dedicated to the business as you are, you might find he would make an ideal assistant manager.

You can also explore job fairs or other standard recruiting opportunities, and even put help wanted signs around your wash. Many top business consultants and recruiting experts will tell you that you should never stop recruiting. Even if you think you're fully staffed, it can never hurt to hire an employee who can help you grow your business.

How to Hire the Best Employees

Now that you know where to look for employees, let's talk about how to hire the best people you can find. After reading the sections above, you should have a good idea of the traits you're looking for. Use that as the basis to write a job description. Not only will this help an applicant know if he or she is qualified for the position, it will also help you evaluate each candidate. If you're simply flying by the seat of your pants, you'll probably tend to overlook an important point here or there—add up all those mistakes and eventually you're going to have one sorry work force.

Identify the pros and cons of each position. It's important to be upfront with your potential employees. No one wants to come into a job expecting the possibility of a promotion only to find out six months later that none exists. Similarly, if you're open to the possibility of an employee moving up the chain in your organization, point that out. It can be a powerful selling point and one that can help sway qualified candidates to work for you as opposed to taking a dead-end job in another field.

You also want to be as honest as you can about the hours and work required. If hard, physical labor is required, tell them right away. If they're going to be standing in a tunnel hosing down cars, they're going to want to know that before they show up for their first day of work. It's also important to be clear about what they will be paid and how you plan to operate your review process—i.e., when they will be eligible for a raise and what it will take for them to get there.

Take some time to think about how you'll advertise your job openings. You're going to want some way to screen out candidates who aren't qualified right off the bat. If you

Under the Table—Not!

The public often seems to think that car washes are full of employees who are "off the books." You may assume that paying employees under the table is a convenient escape from the paperwork and regulations you have to wade through to hire someone legally. You might be tempted to take the easy way out and employ a few nonessential employees in this manner. So here's a word of advice: Don't!

The headaches you might avoid by hiring employees illegally are nothing compared to the headaches you'll suffer if you're ever caught. For example, an employee who works for you off the books can, at just about any time, turn you in. If this happens, not only will you pay fines, but you'll be required to pay all the back taxes you should have paid—plus interest for the time that employee worked for you. It's even worse if one of these employees gets hurt on the job.

As one car wash owner puts it: "When you keep an employee off the books, you have a silent partner." Why? How can you fire or reprimand one of these employees when you know how easy it can be for them to get you in serious trouble with the government? It's almost like you're asking them to blackmail you. They have you over a barrel, and that's a position no business owner wants to be in.

can take a quick look at a resume, or spend five minutes on the phone with someone, it's better than having to drop what you're doing for a half-hour interview with someone you're likely to reject.

Once you've been in business for a while, you'll probably start to see a pattern—perhaps most of your best employees come from the local community college, for example. If that's the case, now you can possibly forego the cost of advertising and work with the college to post job openings.

You can also use your existing employees as recruiters. Many companies offer incentives to their employees to bring qualified people into the business. Perhaps you could offer a $50 bonus to any employee who brings a worker to you after that person has worked with you for a certain period of time, say three months. This can be a great strategy, as long as you have good employees in the first place, of course.

Overcoming the Dead-End Job Stigma

Let's face it. Most kids do not grow up wanting to be car wash employees. Doctors, nurses, firemen, baseball players? Yes. A service writer at a car wash? Not likely. Whether it's deserved or not, the car wash industry certainly suffers from the perception that jobs in the industry are mostly of the low-paying, dead-end variety. In fact, ask most people on the street and they'd probably put these jobs somewhere near being an overnight janitor on the great-jobs-to-have ladder. This is a stigma that you, as a car wash owner, are going to have to overcome.

A good way to start is by breaking through some of the common myths about jobs in the car wash industry. Then you'll be able to communicate a positive attitude to your prospective hires.

- *Myth #1: All car wash jobs are low-paying.* This really depends on what you mean by low pay. Someone who is used to making minimum wage will view a job that pays $.50 an hour more than minimum wage as one that pays pretty well. If a cashier at your local McDonald's starts out making $8 an hour and one at the local Wal-Mart makes $8.25, Wal-Mart would be the place to work. But chances are, you'll never hear anyone talking about how much those Wal-Mart cashiers are pulling down every week. The point is that low pay is a relative concept—assuming that you're paying at least as much as what other companies are paying for similar work. In terms of positions such as service writer or assistant manager, the pay in these positions can be quite good compared to similar positions in other types of businesses, especially if these employees are being compensated in some manner that is commensurate with the profits of your business.

- *Myth #2: Car wash jobs offer no opportunity for advancement.* It's fairly common for employees to start on the bottom rung in a car wash and move up to a position such as service writer within a reasonable time. It doesn't happen overnight, nor does it happen overnight in other industries. What you should be promoting to your employees is that the opportunities are there to advance, and advance quickly, through hard work and dedication to the business.

To sum up, you should maximize the advantages of working in the car wash industry when you are hiring new job applicants, as well as to retain the employees you already have. You need to make it clear that employees at your car wash have the opportunity to earn tips, to advance, and to work in a fun and challenging environment.

How Do You Retain Employees?

We're all motivated by different forces. For some people, simply the satisfaction in knowing that they've done a job well is enough. For others, praise might be a motivator. But one thing just about everyone is motivated by is—you guessed it—money. We've already talked in general terms about the need to compensate your employees fairly, lest you run the risk of creating a revolving door powered by an unmotivated and surly lot of employees who your customers may dread encountering on your lot.

But base pay is really only one part of the equation. There's also the question of incentives—those little perks you offer that allow employees to boost their compensation above and beyond their standard pay. Lots of car wash owners have some type of

A Unique Tip

Instead of distributing tips at the end of each day or week, try a different and unique approach. Put them in a savings account, let them grow and earn interest, and then distribute them at the end of the year—possibly as a holiday bonus. This has a couple of advantages. For one thing, it builds the amount of money your employees earn because they'll be earning interest on the money all year long. For another, it might help slow the revolving door of employees by giving your workers an extra incentive to stick around (at least until the end of the year). To make sure the money is distributed fairly, you should come up with a simple formula that compensates workers based on the number of hours or shifts that they worked during the year. You can even post a bulletin board or poster that tracks contributions to the tip fund and shows their value every other week (or month, or whatever you choose).

incentive program for their employees, since it allows owners to motivate employees by tying their financial success directly to the success of the business. But in order for this to work, you have to design your program so that it has maximum impact.

What Do You Want Your Incentive Program to Accomplish?

The first step seems obvious, but it's one that is sometimes ignored. In order for any incentive program to work, you have to know what it is you're trying to accomplish— what it is you're asking employees to do. For example, increasing revenue is certainly always a goal for any business, but it's not really something specific enough to ask your employees to work for. Rather than a broad, general goal that your employees will have trouble quantifying, you might try offering incentives tied to the number of super-duper-grand-deluxe washes your service writers sell.

Think about the difference that makes. If your employee knows he is going to get $1 for every customer who orders your most expensive wash, he's going to do his best to up-sell. If, instead, he's working toward some vague notion of increasing revenues for the company (without any real concrete idea of exactly how it benefits him) that same motivation might not be there. You could also offer a flat bonus to an employee who exceeds a certain level of sales or sells a certain number of high-priced packages. Another option might be to offer a percentage of the sales or a percentage of sales once receipts reach a certain level. These options are a bit more complicated than the simple "one wash, one buck" system, but they still let the employee know that their success is tied to how well the business does.

There are other areas that you might want to target for incentive programs. Customer service is an important one. These can be a bit harder to administer because the concept of good customer service is somewhat subjective. You can try things like comment cards, but these might turn out to be a bit unwieldy to deal with. You can also try to simply evaluate the general level of service you see over a certain period of time, and distribute "bonuses" to all your line workers based on how you feel they've performed over the past week or month. Another option would be to use your creativity in developing a program everyone can understand. For example, maybe you could put $10 into a fund for every day that is free of customer complaints, and then distribute the money at the end of every month to all your employees, based on how much they worked that month

If you offer incentives, remember that they have to be large enough to mean something to your employees. The bottom line is that you're

Smart Tip

When scouting the competition, pay particular attention to the service you receive. If an employee stands out in your mind as being exceptional, offer him a dollar more an hour to come work for you. You can never have too many good employees.

asking your employees to work harder so that your business does better financially. Show them you appreciate the effort and share the wealth. Think of it this way: If your employees can increase sales by 2 percent, even if you gave them back 15 percent of that, you'd still be ahead.

Offer Health Insurance and Benefits

Ask most car wash owners and they'll tell you that, more and more, they're finding it essential to offer benefits to their employees to attract the kind of competent, reliable employees they need. Medical and dental insurance are often at the top of the list of desired benefits. It's no secret that this can get incredibly expensive, so it will definitely pay to shop around to see if you can scare up any deals.

One avenue you might want to look into is getting insurance through a local organization that you belong to. A logical choice would be your chamber of commerce. You can also try national organizations such as the National Federation of Independent Business. Once you're a member, you may be eligible to buy insurance at a reduced rate.

Training Programs

Your employees, unless they have some previous car wash experience, are probably going to come to you completely green. Everything they know about the car wash business is going to come from you. This means you're going to need a training program. Keep these guidelines in mind as you design one:

- *Don't simply teach how; also teach why.*
- *Define objectives clearly.*
- *Lead by example.*

Technical Training

To begin with, your employees need to be taught how everything works. You don't need to teach them enough so that they're going to know how to fix the machinery in a pinch (though that would be nice, wouldn't it?). But they should have a working knowledge of the basic process involved in washing a car and how to spot small problems before they become big ones.

For a full-service or exterior-conveyor wash, any training program you initiate should include a walk through your tunnel (when it's not operating, of course), during which you can point out the various pieces of equipment, what they do when they're working properly, and what they might do if they malfunction. For a self-service or in-bay automatic wash, you're going to want to take them into your equipment room and around the bays and machinery to demonstrate the process.

Customer Service Training

This may be even more important than the technical stuff. Unfortunately, dealing with people in a respectful and helpful way doesn't come naturally to some people. We're talking about employees who may be very dedicated to their work, but who, for one reason or another, aren't the best when it comes to dealing with customers. If you have enough of these employees, you may have the smoothest-running car wash in town with the least volume of cars actually passing through it.

Training your people to be great with customers doesn't just mean requiring that they greet every customer with a "Good morning, welcome to Al's car wash"—although that's certainly a start. It also means teaching them how to listen to customers and to follow through when a complaint is made. One of the difficulties here is that this directive will sometimes contradict your other major goal—to wash as many cars as possible.

Let's face it, it will be rare that every day will simply involve running cars through your wash, collecting customers' money, and sending them on their way. There are going to be problems that have to be resolved, problems that will eat up some of your time and resources that could otherwise be spent making money. But you can't think of it that way and neither can your employees. Remember, it's much, much cheaper to hold

---

Can We Talk?

There's nothing like a busy conveyor wash. The first time you see a long line of cars stretching from the entrance to your tunnel, you're going to know why you got into this business in the first place. But with your good fortune come a few problems that you're going to have to solve. One of these is communication. What's the best way to relay information from your service writers, who may be busily working taking orders far away from the tunnel, to the technicians who are actually operating the equipment? It sounds like a minor detail, but it's a vitally important question. If your employees are messing up orders, it can create confusion and a slowdown, resulting in lost customers and profits.

For this reason, give some thought to what the best way would be for your employees to talk to each other and relay information about customers on your busiest days. Some washes use a simple bar of soap to write orders on a customer's windshield. You can also try washable or dry-erase markers to accomplish the same thing. Another way to do it, if you're a bit leery about writing on your customer's cars, is to give each of your service writers a kind of ticket book. They can write orders on the tickets and place them under the windshield for your other employees to see.

> **Beware!**
> Be careful about who you hire as an employee. One owner told us a story about an employee who broke equipment on purpose so that he would get overtime to fix it.

on to existing customers than it is to go out and replace customers who won't become regulars because of a bad experience they had at your wash. Instead, your employees must be trained to treat each customer complaint or concern with seriousness.

Your employees should be trained to recognize that a complaint is not a bad thing in all circumstances—instead, it's an opportunity to create a truly satisfied customer. Don't get us wrong, we're not saying you should intentionally solicit complaints from customers. But what we are encouraging you to do is to not necessarily view them as a bad thing. On the contrary, there can often be nothing more satisfying than doing your best to please an unhappy customer and turning him around from a liability to an asset.

So train your employees to welcome all comments—positive and negative. Give them an idea of common customer service complaints they'll encounter and how to resolve them. Give them the power to make things right when a customer isn't happy. Heck, give them a $5 bonus every time they bring a complaint to you. Whatever it takes to ensure that you do whatever you can to have every customer leave your wash happy, satisfied, and ready to spread the word about your great business.

Turning Over Responsibilities

There's probably going to come a time when you decide to turn over the day-to-day managerial responsibilities of your wash to one of your employees. That's not a guarantee—you might love the work so much that you can't imagine someone else doing it—but if you decide to open another wash, take a vacation, or simply retire from the daily grind, someone is going to have to step in and do all of the mundane things you've been handling.

How do you decide which of your employees will get the keys to the shop? Here are some of the characteristics you should look for in anyone you are considering selecting as a managerial employee to fill in for you:

- *Financial responsibility.* Most of your business is transacted in cash. It's very easy for some of it to go missing if it's not in the right hands.
- *Respect of the other employees.* Employees must treat the manager with the same respect they show you.

> **Smart Tip**
> Always maintain a list of on-call workers to replace any regularly scheduled workers who don't show up for their shift.

- *Respect of the customers.* If customers have gotten to know the employee and like him, they won't hesitate to remain loyal to your business.
- *Honesty.* You need to know that if your manager tells you something happened, it's as good as if you saw it happen with your own eyes.
- *Ambition.* A good manager wants to prove to you, and to himself, that he can do a good job running the business.
- *Attention to detail.* You built your business by making sure everything ran like a well-oiled machine. Someone needs to pay as close attention to the little things as you did.
- *Dependability.* This is a trait that the employee you're considering should have displayed over the entire time he spent working for you.

There may be other factors that play into your decision, too. It could be that you don't think any of your existing employees fit the bill, and you have to go outside to find a manager. You can try luring away an experienced car wash manager from another business by promising a bit more money. That may work, but remember this: If he joined you for more money, he could also leave you for more money. Then you'd be right back at square one.

Whatever you decide, it's important that you're extremely comfortable with the decision you make. Nothing is worse than lying in bed at night wondering how well your business is being run.

Knowing When to Let Them Go

There probably isn't a business in the United States that hasn't had to fire an employee at some time or another, and your car wash probably isn't going to be any different. Firing someone is never a pleasant task, but if you're going to run a business, you're going to have learn how to do it correctly to safeguard yourself.

We live in a litigious country. If you can sue a fast-food restaurant for millions of dollars—and win—because you spilled a cup of coffee on yourself, how often do you think employers are sued for wrongful termination?

A comprehensive employee manual will give you some protection in the form of backup that the employee had knowledge of what conduct was expected of him. If you follow your reprimand schedule in your manual, or adhere to your requirements for what constitutes an "on-the-spot" firing, you're in a much better situation than if you appear to be acting on a whim. It's pretty hard for employees to complain that they were fired incorrectly if you can document a clear violation of the rules as set out in writing in the employee manual. What actually determines when it's time to fire an employee is pretty much up to your discretion, but the point is that it should be done following a set of guidelines that you've set down and of which your employees are well aware. Take a look

Stat Fact
The average full-service wash employs just over 30 people in a given year.

at the section "Developing Your Employee Manual" (below) for elements to include in your employee manual.

How should you conduct what's come to be known as "the exit interview"? In a word: carefully. Remember, you're not trying to create an enemy here. You certainly don't want someone with an inside knowledge of your business to hold a serious grudge against you. You can offer to help them find a job somewhere else where their skills might be more appropriate or make clear that you won't give a blanket negative recommendation to any potential employer who calls. Of course, you don't want to lie on the former employee's behalf, but you can let him know you don't intend to make it hard for him to hook up with another company.

Developing Your Employee Manual

Despite what popular misconceptions lead us to believe, hiring a car wash employee entails a lot more than just tossing a few dry rags at someone and telling them to get to work. Employees need to be taught both what is expected of them, as well as behavior that won't be tolerated. This is important not just because it helps your business run more smoothly, but because it can also save you the headache of a lawsuit if an employee feels he or she was fired for no good reason. One way to accomplish this is with a well-thought-out employee manual. You'll probably want to consult an attorney about exactly what kinds of things should go into your employee manual, but here are some ideas to get you started.

- *Wash processes.* Describe in detail exactly what happens when a car disappears into the tunnel, if you're running a full-service or exterior-conveyor wash, or the process for washing a car yourself if you're running a self-service wash. When employees know what's going on, they're better prepared to assist customers if they have any questions or if something goes wrong.

- *The equipment.* Explain what the equipment does and how it works. You don't need to go into the kind of detail a mechanic would need, but a general overview of how the equipment functions can help an employee spot potential problems and also answer basic customer questions.

- *Your menu of services.* This may change a bit from time to time as you expand

Beware!
When you find it necessary to discipline employees, make sure you document everything that is said and save it. This can help prevent complaints and lawsuits later on if you find it necessary to terminate their employment.

into other areas or drop services that aren't contributing to your profits, but you should be able to give a general overview of the services you provide. Break each level of service down, and explain each of the components.

- *Your mission statement or philosophy.* Perhaps nothing is more important for your employees to know, at least in terms of conveying what your business is all about, than your mission statement. There's almost no doubt that you'll have this information posted in other places besides your employee manual, but there's no reason why it shouldn't be part of this document as well.

- *Customer payment.* It's probably a good idea to let all of your employees know (i.e., not just the cashier) what forms of payment you accept and how the various forms of payment are processed. A customer might ask any employee about your policy on accepting credit cards, personal checks, or traveler's checks. Employees should also know the procedure for redeeming gift certificates and what to do in case a credit card is rejected.

- *Customer complaints.* Spell out exactly what is expected of an employee who receives a customer complaint. Who should be notified? How should it be handled? By explaining the process now, you reduce the chance of a conflict down the road. No one wants to have a customer play one employee off another, or an employee off a manager or owner, when it comes to the subject of paying for damages or providing extra service. Having everyone on the same page will help to lessen the chances of that happening.

- *Tipping or commission policy.* For most of your employees, tips or other forms of nonsalaried payment are probably going to be part of their compensation. Take the opportunity to spell out the program in your employee manual (though you'll probably want to have another document that goes into even greater detail).

- *Uniforms and appearance.* Assuming that your employees will be required to be in uniform (and they should be), you will need to spell out exactly what it means when you say they must show up to work "in uniform." For example, for an employee considered to be in proper uniform, you may want to stress that his or her uniform must be clean. You should also state at least some basic policy about jewelry, facial hair, and personal hygiene.

- *Employee absenteeism.* You should make it clear that employees are expected to show up for work on time when they're scheduled. If they can't make a shift, you might want to require that they find somebody else to cover for them.

- *Employee scheduling.* Tell your employees how the scheduling system works, as well as where and when the schedule is posted each week. This section might also include your policy on schedule requests and vacations—i.e., how requests are made, how the manager or owner determines whether to deny or accept the request, etc.

- *Harassment policy.* This is one you're almost definitely going to need a lawyer to help you with, but here's the point you should be striving to make: No employee will at any time harass another employee, customer or vendor. This includes sexual harassment. There's no room for ambiguity here. Make clear what steps employees should take if they feel they are being harassed (i.e., who should be notified about the incident, what steps will be taken, etc.). You should also indicate what steps will be taken against the offending party if the complaint is found to have merit (this will in all likelihood be immediate termination).

- *Reprimand schedule.* One of the ways to protect yourself against claims that an employee was terminated unfairly is to spell out in specific detail how you plan to reprimand employees who break the rules. Once you have spelled out exactly how you expect employees to perform their duties, the next step is to let them know what will happen if they don't live up to your standards. A typical reprimand schedule might be a verbal warning for the first violation, followed by a written warning and perhaps the loss of a shift (or some other "pocketbook penalty") for a second violation. A third violation would most likely result in termination. Again, this is an area where you should consult an attorney, but those are some general guidelines many businesses follow.

- *Termination policy.* This section should cover not only what constitutes grounds for termination, but also what you expect if the employee decides to quit. Although there's really no way to enforce it, you should require that employees give at least ten days' notice that they'll be leaving. This will give you enough time to shift your schedule to ensure that you don't wind up short on busy days. You can probably increase the likelihood that an employee will honor the notice

> **Y**ou should require that employees give at least ten days' notice that they'll be leaving.

period by making it clear that any positive recommendations to future employers are dependent on the employee leaving your business on good terms.

- *Drug policy.* This is certainly another area where an attorney can help you draft language that protects you. Aside from the legalese you'll most likely have to insert in this section, the main point you want to get across is that showing up for work while under the influence of alcohol or drugs is grounds for immediate termination. This is important not only because of the image your employees project to your customers, but for safety reasons as well. Obviously, an employee under the influence is much more likely to hurt himself or others than one who shows up clean and sober.

- *Discount policy.* As an added perk, you may want to grant free or reduced wash privileges for your employees. You can also extend that privilege to immediate

▲

family members if you're feeling generous. If you decide to offer this, you're probably going to want to set limits. For instance, you certainly don't want your employee's mother, father, and brother showing up on a busy Saturday morning for a free wash, thus taking attention away from your paying customers. Perhaps you can limit the discount to a particular day of the week which experience has shown to consistently be your slowest day. You'll also want to limit the number of times the discount can be used—twice a month for example.

- *Equal opportunity statement.* A simple statement to the effect that your business does not discriminate on the basis of sex, religion, race, disability, or sexual preference will probably suffice for this section, although your attorney should be the final word here.

- *Other points to cover.* Other sections of your manual might include an employee smoking policy (where and when it's allowed, if at all), what sections of your wash are off limits except to managers (equipment rooms or the office, for example), your policy on taking items from the business (towels, supplies, etc.), and the procedure for making recommendations or lodging complaints with a manager.

Income and
Expenses

Finally! Now we're going to talk specifically about how much money you can make in this business. There is a very specific process for determining your anticipated revenue. It involves lots of number-crunching and research, but it's an absolutely vital part of the process for finding out whether or not your new business will be able to survive.

To some extent, the decision on whether or not to proceed with your specific car wash business is a subjective one. The so-called fringe benefits of owning your own business may be paramount in your mind, and as long as you can make a living doing it, that may be enough. But usually you're going to want to get a bit more out of it. In addition, assuming that you're going to need a loan to get started, the bank will want to see that you're going to be able to survive financially before it grants your loan.

Evaluating Risk

Investing in anything involves some amount of risk. Contrary to what many people believe, the definition of risk is a lot broader than what you may think. For example, it's easy to see what the risk is when you invest in the stock of an unproven, highly speculative new company. Following that train of thought, you'd probably say that it's a bit less risky to invest in a blue-chip stock, safer still to invest in government bonds, and virtually foolproof to invest in a bank certificate of deposit, or simply to keep your money in a savings account. That's the way most people look at risk. But in economic terms that's not entirely accurate, and here's why. When you tie your money up in a low-yield investment such as a CD, you're risking your ability to earn higher returns through another form of investment. What all this means is that even what you may consider to be the safest investment, may turn out to cost you money in the long run. If you think of it in those terms, you will start to get a better feel for just how risk-tolerant you are.

For now though, let's stick with the generally accepted definition of risk. The less sure you are about how an investment will perform, the riskier it is. Opening your own car wash business lies somewhere near the risky end of the spectrum.

One of the reasons interest rates on bank savings accounts are so low is because there is so little risk involved. Banks can get away with paying 4, 3, or even 2 percent interest because there's virtually no chance you'll lose money. It's a whole different ballgame when you're starting a new business. You're going to be looking for a much higher return on your investment to justify the risk involved.

Your Rate of Return

Exactly what your desired rate of return should be depends on many factors, some of which can't really be quantified (such as being your own boss). But beyond those, there are some hard and fast numbers that you'll have to consider before you jump in. For this analysis, you'll need to know how much money you can hope to make, what you're going to have to pay to make that income, and the size of your initial investment.

Except for your initial investment, you're going to have to make an educated guess about the other numbers. You can use charts on pages 120–122 as sample estimates.

Projecting Annual Revenue from an Existing Wash

If you've done your homework, you should have a pretty decent idea of how much money you can expect to take in every year. You may want to be a bit conservative in coming up with this number. Being too optimistic can lead you into making an investment in an existing wash that will be very hard to keep afloat.

If you're buying an existing wash, the current owner is probably going to be your best source of information for the kind of revenue you can expect. Be careful about assuming that, once you take over and make improvements, you're going to be able to dramatically increase revenue over the previous owner. Experience says otherwise. Sure, if you upgrade and modernize your equipment or clean up the exterior of the facility, you may see a slight bump in revenue—but nothing dramatic.

If you have reason to suspect that the numbers you're seeing from the current owner have been "fudged," there are ways to check their validity using other information. One way is to check water usage records for the business. Once you know how much water the site is using, you can call the equipment manufacturer to get a rough estimate of the volume of business the site should be doing. It's not an exact measure of course, but it can give you an indication as to whether or not you're getting accurate figures from the current owner.

Projecting Annual Revenue from a New Wash

This is a bit trickier. To get an accurate picture of what you can expect to make from a new wash that you'll build from scratch, you're going to need information from a wide variety of sources. First and foremost is data from places such as the International Carwash Association (ICA). It can provide you with information such as average annual revenues and costs for a variety of different types of washes across the country. There are also ways you can check into this kind of information on your own.

This means driving around to various car washes in your area and simply checking out the pricing. For a full-service, exterior-conveyor, or in-bay automatic wash, all you need to do is check out the car wash's menu of services. For a self-service wash, you may need to do a bit more investigating. You aren't simply looking at price; you're also looking at time. How much time in the bay does each token or each quarter buy the customer? By taking the price and dividing it by the time of the cycle, you come up with a figure that represents how much a customer is paying for a minute of washing time. That's the figure you'll want to use for projecting revenues.

Pick a pricing schedule that lies somewhere in the middle of the prices you've seen other washes charge. This will help ensure that you aren't being overly optimistic about your chances.

The next step is to determine the volume you can expect. Again, organizations such as the ICA can provide data that can help with this calculation. You can also make use of figures you obtain independently.

For a self-service wash, what you'll want to know is how many minutes a day (on average) you can expect each bay to be in operation. This will vary from region to region, as well as from location to location. Based on surveys in publications such as *Professional Carwashing & Detailing* magazine and *Auto Laundry News*, the average minutes a day can range from less than 100 to more than 150. You can try to obtain some numbers of car wash owners in your region, as long as they are far enough away from your new site to not see you as a competitor. If you survey enough of these, you'll probably be able to come up with a fairly good estimate.

Let's take a number in the middle and say that, based on your research and independent numbers you've studied from surveys, you're assuming you can reasonably

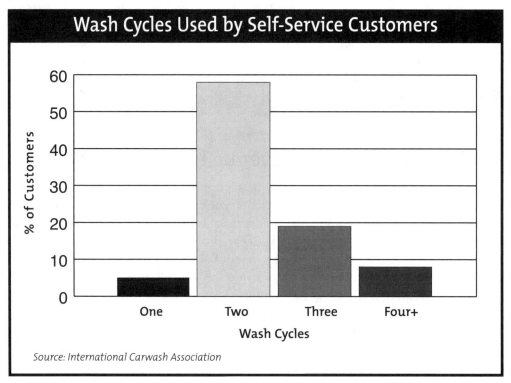

Wash Cycles Used by Self-Service Customers

Source: International Carwash Association

Stat Fact
Two-thirds of self-service owners have never accepted credit cards as a payment option, according to a report from the International Carwash Association.

expect each of your bays to be in operation for 125 minutes a day. Multiply that by the price per minute you can expect to receive—perhaps $.40—and you come up with a figure that will tell you how much revenue you can expect each of your bays to generate on a daily basis. In this example it would be $50 a day. Multiply that by 365 to find your annual revenue for each bay. Using the numbers we have here, that would work out to $18,250 in annual revenue per bay. Finally, multiply that by the number of bays you plan to build, and you'll have the total annual washing revenue for each bay. If you plan to open a six-bay wash, your total annual revenue would be $109,500.

Now it's time to move on to your other profit centers, such as vacuuming, vending machines, etc. A conservative estimate might be that revenue from these sources will amount to about 15 percent of the revenue you receive from actually washing cars. In the example we've been using, that would come to $16,425. Add this figure to the revenue generated from washing operations and you come up with $125,925 in total revenue. Still with us?

The process for determining projected revenue for other types of washes is similar. You're going to need to know how much volume you can expect, but instead of estimating the number of minutes a day your wash will be in operation, you're going to want to know how many cars you can expect to wash in any given year. This again will vary depending on your region, but surveys can give some indication of averages.

For an in-bay automatic wash—the kind you might typically find as a supplement to a self-service wash—a recent survey in *Auto Laundry News* put the average number of cars washed annually in each automatic bay at 21,337. For the purposes of streamlining an example, let's round that off to 20,000. Again, this is a general average compiled from owners all across the country. Let's also assume that your wash has three automatic bays so that the total number of cars you can expect to wash in any given year is around 60,000.

Next, rather than the price per minute you expect to charge, you'll need to know the revenue you can expect to generate from each car. The average gross revenue for each in-bay customer, according to *Auto Laundry News*, is $4.48. Again rounding off for our example, let's make it $4.50. This means that your wash will generate $90,000 in revenue per bay every year. If you have three bays, the total revenue comes to $270,000.

For exterior-conveyor and full-service washes, the process for arriving at projected revenue is pretty much the same, but the numbers change. While it's a little harder to arrive at an average for the number of cars you can expect to wash, the greatest number of respondents for both exterior-conveyor and full-service washes in a recent survey by *Auto Laundry News* said they washed between 20,000 and 35,000 cars in a year. According to the survey, 75 percent of the exterior-conveyor owners surveyed said they made between $4 and $7 average gross revenue per car, while most owners of full-service washes said they could expect to make between $9 and $12 a car. If you expect to wash around 27,000 cars for either an exterior-conveyor or full-service wash, you can estimate that you will take in around $5.50 average gross revenue per car for an exterior-conveyor wash and around $10.50 a car for a full-service wash. Based on these numbers, you'll arrive at a projected annual revenue of $148,500 for an exterior-conveyor wash and $283,500 for a full-service wash.

Remember that in all these examples we're figuring out average revenue a day. This doesn't mean that you can expect to make this every day. It simply means that at the end of the year, when you add up all the totals, this is the average of what you

A Token Thought

The choice of whether or not to use tokens or money to operate your machinery is a pretty big one, and unfortunately there's no great consensus about which is better. You'll find owners who swear by tokens, just as you'll find owners who swear by sticking with cash. Here are some of the pros and cons of each approach.

If you stick with coins, anecdotal evidence suggests that you'll have more incidents of vandalism, since crooks have a lot more to gain by stealing real money rather than phony money that can only be used at your wash.

However, some owners say that the drop in vandalism simply isn't worth losing customers. While there are no hard and fast statistics to back it up, these owners say that they've heard about washes that switched from coins to tokens and lost a significant amount of business—business that never came back, even when they went back to using coins.

On the other side of the coin (pun intended), tokens, in addition to cutting down on the kind of vandalism that can really cripple your wash, can make it easy to market your business. Here's why: Say, for example, that you want to try a marketing tactic like pursuing premium deals (see page 134) or working with a charity. It's very easy to simply sell your tokens at a discount to a third-party, which they in turn can resell to the eventual end-user. If you're operating under a cash system, you don't have the opportunity for this kind of arrangement—you can't sell a quarter at a discount. So if concerns over safety and the "portability" of your marketing efforts are high on your list, tokens may be the way to go.

made on any given day during the year. There will be slow days (and slow weeks and months), just as there will be days when you get "slammed." This is an important distinction, especially if you're making loan payments that come due every month. Try telling the bank that you can't make a payment on your loan because it's your "slow time of the year." Good luck.

Operating Costs

Now that we have a handle on projected revenues, we need to study operating costs. Then, finally, we'll have an idea of the kind of profit-making potential your car wash will have.

How much do you estimate it will cost to run your business? Unlike the conservative approach you should take when projecting revenues, it's probably a better idea to err on the high side when estimating costs. Take everything into account here—employees, general supplies, maintenance, legal fees, insurance, etc.

For an existing car wash, this is pretty simple. Take a look at the books, and this will tell you (give or take a couple of percent) what your costs are going to be. Of course, if you plan on making radical changes, such as upgrading equipment, hiring or firing a significant number of employees, or radically changing the menu of services, you're going to have to factor that into the equation.

For Example...

To illustrate what we've already discussed, we're going to give you some examples of what a typical business's monthly income/expense statement might look like. Take a look at the charts on pages 120–122. They outline three examples: a full-service wash, an exterior-conveyor wash, and a self-service/in-bay automatic combo.

Remember, these numbers are averages. Your income and expenses will vary depending on many factors, including where in the country your wash is located, for example. Generally, both income and expenses will be lower in rural areas and higher as you move closer to major urban areas.

What you can take from these examples is that your monthly income and expenses are going to be higher as you move from a small self-serve-only location up the ladder to a full-service wash. Of course, as your revenue

Smart Tip

Tip...

If you're constructing a brand-new self-service wash, try to construct your bays so that the openings have southern exposure. This will keep them warmer during cold periods, thus helping to prevent ice buildup, while simultaneously keeping down your heating costs.

113

▲

and expenses increase, so will the work required to run your business. If the thought of dealing in millions of dollars rather than thousands gives you pause, jumping in with both feet and owning a full-service wash at the get-go probably isn't the best idea.

Calculating Your Return on Investment

For this exercise you're going to need to know the size of your initial investment (i.e., how much it's going to cost to start or buy your car wash business), the projected operating costs for the business, and the projected revenue for the business.

Knowing these three things, you can now calculate what your expected annual rate of return, or return on investment (ROI), will be. You can determine this figure as follows:

- *Step 1.* Subtract projected costs from projected revenue. This gives you your estimated annual profit.
- *Step 2.* Divide your estimated annual profit by the amount of money you're going to invest. This is your ROI.
- *Example.* Consider a hypothetical four-bay, self-serve wash where you invest $100,000.

  Projected revenue = four bays x $15,000 a year = $60,000

  Projected costs = supplies and maintenance (4 bays x $5,000 a year) = $20,000

  Miscellaneous expenses (legal fees, insurance, etc.) = $12,000

  Projected profit = $60,000 − $32,000 = $28,000

  Return on investment = $28,000 ÷ $100,000 = 0.28 (or 28 percent) ROI (pretty darn good)

It's important to point out that there's no right or wrong answer here. A 10 percent ROI might be all right for some, but too low for others. What determines your own personally acceptable ROI will depend on factors such as the other investment options available to you and the nonmonetary benefits you'll derive from being in business for yourself. Of course, if your ROI is zero or close to it, that's a bad idea no matter how much of a thrill you'll get from being your own boss.

Revenue Streams

We hope this will come as no surprise: The vast majority of your revenue will come from washing cars. However, most car wash owners today supplement that income by providing other goods or services. These additional revenue streams can be vitally important. For example, some statistics put revenue from vending machines at around 15 percent of the total revenue for a self-service wash, while some put it even higher.

That's pretty dramatic. For an idea of just how much this can affect your business, just think what would happen if you watched your revenue drop 15 percent in a year.

Extra services can take the form of anything from vending machines to vacuum or shampooing facilities. While it's important to recognize that the wash is your main service, don't get so focused on that aspect of the business that you lose sight of the many other profit centers available to you.

Vending Machines

We were hard-pressed to find any self-service owners who didn't have vending machines on their lot. There's a reason for this. A vending machine is probably just about the easiest money you're going to make. All you have to do is keep it stocked.

The majority of the owners we spoke with advised new car wash owners not to skimp when it comes to installing vending machines. Look for a large, glass-door model that will allow you to display a variety of products—from food and drinks to car-related items such as air fresheners.

Vacuum Services

Like vending machines, offering vacuum services can be yet another source of revenue (assuming that you're not running a full-service wash, since you'll more than likely be providing these services as part of your wash package already). Again, as with vending machines, owners we spoke with encouraged new owners to install vacuums on their site. How many is up to you, but you don't want to have only one vacuum if

---

Numbers Talk

How much will you earn as a car wash owner? The numbers here vary greatly depending on a number of factors, including the size of your facility and your location. In general, here are some numbers to give you a rough idea of what to expect:

❍ *Self-service*   average monthly gross income a bay = $1,200 to $1,700

❍ *In-bay automatic*   average monthly gross income a bay = $3,500 to $4,500

❍ *Exterior-conveyor*   average monthly gross income = $27,000 to $40,000

❍ *Full-service*   average monthly gross income = $55,000 to $75,000

▲

you're operating a six-bay self-serve. Perhaps one a bay, or just slightly fewer than that (five vacuums for a six-bay wash, for example), is a good rule of thumb.

Gift Shops

Depending on the space you have available, you may be able to combine your wash with a small gift shop. For example, Dick H. in Sacramento, California, doesn't just sell air fresheners and fuzzy dice for your rearview mirror in his shop. He sells greeting cards (even claiming to have one of the largest selections in the area) and handbags. It may sound strange, but when you think about it, why should it be? Remember, as we've been discussing, one of the things car wash customers want is to combine getting a wash with other errands. If they can stop for a wash and then run in to pick up a birthday card, why not do it? In the end, you're really only limited by your imagination and your space in terms of what you can sell.

Adding Offline Services

Offline services are services not directly related to washing cars. The range of services you can offer in addition to car washes sometimes seems to have no end. For example, in addition to vending machines with your typical snack foods of chips and soft drinks, some washes have gone to even greater lengths—like setting up a real, bona-fide fast-food restaurant on the premises. While that's an expensive proposition, you could probably think of something similar to do with your wash.

What about hiring a guy to sell hot dogs during lunchtime? Maybe, if you're located in an area that already has street vendors, you could invite one of them to set up shop on your lot and ask for a share of his profits. It helps the vendor because he's taking advantage of your traffic flow and a steady stream of customers. It helps you because you're making a little extra money with no additional effort. And it helps your customers because you're providing them with a service they wouldn't normally expect to find at a car wash.

But it doesn't stop there. Think about what other opportunities your facilities allow you to explore. For example, did you know there's a company that manufactures equipment that will allow your customers to wash their pets in one of your self-service bays? It's true. Now, we're not saying you necessarily want people washing their dogs at your car wash, but the point is that there are a whole host of services you can provide that you may not have thought of. Any product or service that you can provide, perhaps especially if it's a unique, one-of-a-kind service like a pet wash, can help build your business by filling a need that others don't.

Taken together, extras such as vacuums, vending machines, carpet and upholstery cleaning, snack shops, and similar services and products, can dramatically boost your bottom line. How much? The average full-service wash takes in an additional $18,000 every month from nonwash sales. Exterior-conveyor washes make about an extra $7,000 a month. For self-service facilities, vacuums bring in about $1,000 a month, carpet and upholstery cleaning around $100, air fresheners about $200, and soda and snack sales, $250.

Other Automotive Services

Although we're not going to get too far into the subject in this book, there are some other services you can provide if you have the space. Detailing is a logical extension for some car washes, as are quickie oil and lube jobs. Here are some basic considerations that will determine if these services are appropriate for your wash.

- *Space*. Land is expensive. In fact, it'll probably cost you nearly as much to obtain the land for your wash as it will to equip the wash itself. Therefore, it could very well be that adding major offline services is simply cost-prohibitive. If you do have land available for more services, you might want to think about whether that space would better be used for additional wash services—more self-service bays, an in-bay automatic unit, or extra vacuum islands in the case of a full-service wash.

- *Expertise*. Learning the car wash business is hard enough without having to learn about everything that goes into performing other automotive services as well. If you're going to have your hands full learning the ins and outs of running a car wash on a day-to-day basis, you might want to think about whether you're going to have the time, or the inclination, to perform these additional services properly.

- *Employees*. If you're operating a self-service wash and don't plan on hiring any employees, you should realize that by adding additional services such as those mentioned above, you'll almost certainly need to hire workers. If one of the things that attracted you to the car wash business in the first place was that you didn't need to worry about employees and the hassle that goes along with them, you probably aren't going to want to hire employees for services that that aren't part of your core business anyway.

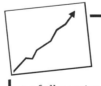

- *Demand.* Is there a demand for the extra services you want to provide? When you were scouting possible locations for your car wash, you took into account lots of information. One element was competition. You'll now have to go through that process again to determine if there's enough demand and a sufficient lack of competition in your area to provide the extra services you're considering.

Should You Lease Your Extra Space?

We've already talked about the need to have adequate space for the type of wash you want to construct, but what if, after you do all of your analysis and build a wash the community will support, you are in the enviable position of having too much space? There are any number of things you can do—build a small store, add vacuum islands, etc. But another option is to lease the space to someone else.

For example, what if your research indicates that a quick lube, oil change, or detailing service is in demand in your area, but you don't want to run it? It might be possible for you to essentially rent the space to someone who does want to run it. Some owners have done just that. If you're serious about trying it, you can make an attempt to raid a local Jiffy-Lube or similar outfit for an experienced manager to run it—someone who lacks the resources to go into business for himself.

You can work out the financial details in a number of different ways. One way would be to lease the space outright. This is a good idea if you're looking for a steady stream of income every month, no matter how much business your new partner does. You could also structure the agreement so that the tenant simply keeps a percentage of revenue. The disadvantage to this type of arrangement is that you don't know from one month to the next what you're going to take in.

Another idea is to rent out the space as a storage place or small warehouse. Depending on the amount of land you have available, and existing structures that may already be on it, you could lease it to a small auto-repair shop or inspection station.

Whatever you decide, there's simply no reason to allow extra land to go to waste, especially not when there are so many possibilities out there for owners who aren't afraid to be a little creative.

Financial Management

You knew it had to come to this. Yes, you are going to have to spend some time sitting behind a desk and filling out paperwork or hiring someone to do it for you. In the long run, it's going to be very hard for you to succeed without a solid financial plan. Set up some sort of system to track your revenue and expenditures. This can be as low-tech as a notebook or as high-tech as sophisticated accounting software. Whatever works best for you is fine.

At least every month, sit down and figure out all your income and expenses for the previous period. This is perhaps going to be a bit more important for a car wash owner than for someone in a business where most money is received by check or credit card. If you're in that type of business, you might be able to let things slide a bit and reconstruct these numbers based on receipts and statements. But for a car wash owner, someone who's emptying a register (or change machine) every day, keeping a close watch on everything that goes in and out the door is critical.

We discussed the role a good accountant can play in Chapter 5, and it may very well be that hiring one is going to be the best thing for you. If the cost is something that bothers you, consider that your time is also a valuable commodity. Every hour that you spend recording every little detail in a financial ledger is one less hour you have to grow your business.

An accountant can also assist you should you run into any problems with the IRS. No one likes to think about the possibility of being audited, but it certainly does happen. If your books have been professionally maintained, you're probably going to lower the risk of overlooking something important that might result in fines and additional taxes.

This is also an important reason to maintain records from previous years, but certainly not the only one. After all, you can't chart the growth of your business if you aren't tracking its performance over time. You could do this on your own (millions of individual taxpayers already do), but again, an accountant may be able to help you set up a system that's more efficient.

In addition to the legal reasons you want to keep accurate books, there's also a business reason for it. A good system will allow you to see where your business is strong and where it needs some help. It can help you determine if a new profit center is actually adding to your bottom line or just eating up precious resources. It can also help you identify areas where you might be able to cut costs.

Dealing with Taxes

Death and taxes, the two things you can always count on. Another reason for keeping

▲

accurate account of your finances will come on April 15th of every year. In addition to paying your federal taxes, you're going to have to pay state and local taxes as well. Add to those taxes, the taxes you're going to have to pay regularly for your employees, and you've got a potential mess on your hands.

If you can afford it, it probably makes sense to hire an accountant to handle your taxes for you. The tax process for a business can be a real maze, especially if you have employees. An accountant should be able to make sure you do it right and

Monthly Income/Expenses for a Full-Service Wash

	Income	Expense
Car wash services (for an average of 5,583 cars washed a month)	$64,000	
Extra online services (wax coating, rust inhibitor, wheel wash, etc.)	18,000	
Offline products (vending machines, car-care products, etc.)	5,000	
Cleaning supplies		$1,900
Wax or other protectants		700
Miscellaneous car wash supplies		750
Utilities (electric, water, phone, gas)		3,100
Office supplies and upkeep		900
Repairs		2,000
Advertising		1,500
Damage		350
Employees (17 full time @ $7.41 an hour, 13 part time @ $6.50 an hour)		28,000
Lease		6,250
Loan payment		3,000
Total Monthly Expenses		**$48,450**
Gross Monthly Income	**$87,000**	
Net Monthly Income	**$38,550**	

don't leave yourself exposed to penalties because you forgot to make a payment here and there.

The laws are always changing, and an accountant can help you figure out things such as depreciation and legitimate business expenses that most laymen simply won't know. Plus, hiring someone to handle this for you frees up your time for more important things—like dreaming up that new marketing plan. In the next chapter, we'll look into the ins and outs of marketing and advertising for your car wash business.

Monthly Income/Expenses for an Exterior-Conveyor Wash

	Income	Expense
Car wash services (for an average of 5,587 cars washed a month)	$33,750	
Extra online services (wax coating, rust inhibitor, wheel wash, etc.)	7,000	
Offline products (vending machines, car-care products, etc.)	2,500	
Cleaning supplies		$1,300
Wax or other protectants		400
Miscellaneous car wash supplies		450
Utilities (water, electric, gas, phone)		3,000
Office supplies and upkeep		450
Repairs		1,500
Advertising		1,500
Damage		150
Employees (5 full time @ $7.25 an hour, 10 part time @ $6.25 an hour)		8,250
Lease		4,000
Loan payment		2,500
Total Monthly Expenses		**$23,500**
Gross Monthly Income	**$43,250**	
Net Monthly Income	**$19,750**	

Monthly Income/Expenses for a Self-Service/In-Bay Automatic Wash

	Income	Expense
Car wash services (for 2,250 self-service customers and 1,000 in-bay automatic customers a month)	$10,000	
Extra online services (vacuuming, upholstery cleaning, etc.)	1,000	
Offline products (vending machines)	400	
Cleaning supplies		$400
Wax or other protectants		75
Miscellaneous car wash supplies		100
Utilities (water, electric, phone, gas)		1,000
Office supplies and upkeep		25
Repairs		400
Advertising		100
Damage		50
Employees (1 full time @ $9.37 an hour)		1,500
Lease		1,000
Loan payment		1,250
Total Monthly Expenses		**$5,900**
Gross Monthly Income	**$11,400**	
Net Monthly Income	**$5,500**	

Advertising, Marketing, and Public Relations

Most of the decisions that you make
that will affect your chances for success in the car wash business are probably going to be made before you ever set up shop:
location, type of wash, equipment purchases, mission statement, philosophy, etc. How you market your new business, and
how you handle public relations, are two very important factors

that will determine your ongoing success once you open your doors (or turn on the faucets, as the case may be).

You basically have three ways you can differentiate yourself from the competition. You can compete on price, you can compete on services and amenities, or you can market yourself better than anyone else. You'll most likely be doing all three of those things, but marketing yourself well is one of the least expensive ways to build your car counts and your revenue.

Coming Up with a Marketing Plan

Just as you came up with a detailed plan for financing and buying (or building) your wash, you now need to turn your attention to creating a plan for bringing in the customers. There's lots of information about how to create a solid marketing plan in "Advertising and Marketing," Chapter 10, of Entrepreneur's *Start-Up Basics*, so we won't go into too much detail about the process here.

The one thing that's important to remember before you get started is that, depending on the type of car wash you decide to open, you're going to be targeting different customers. As we've mentioned before, a self-service car wash is generally going to attract customers in a lower income bracket than a full-service operation would. Common to all car wash owners is the fact that home washers represent a significant segment of the untapped market for your services. Remember, according to the International Carwash Association (ICA), about 50 percent of the population still chooses to wash their cars at home. When you come up with your marketing plan, focus some of your energy on how you might be able to convince those home washers to abandon their hose and bucket, and turn the task over to a professional.

Direct Mail

The purpose of any marketing campaign is to increase awareness for your business among the people most likely to use your services. In earlier chapters, we've discussed some of the ways to do this, but just about all of them required that a potential customer actually drive by your wash. What if there are hundreds or thousands of potential car wash customers in your area, but none of them know you exist? Maybe you're located on a street that's just a block or two away from where they turn going to work every day. How can you reach these people and pull them into your wash? One of the ways might be through a direct-mail campaign.

Direct mail can work in a number of different ways. The two most likely to succeed for a car wash will probably be joining in a larger coupon mailing or renting specific mailing lists on your own and contacting potential customers with information about the services you provide. Let's start with the first type—the large coupon mailing.

Just about every community is served by a company that does massive bulk mailing of coupons for businesses in the area. You've probably received these mailings yourself. Typically, they'll come in a large envelope and contain maybe two dozen coupons for everything from eyeglasses to movie rentals. Why not try adding some coupons for your car wash? This does two things right away. First, it captures those people we've been talking about—the ones who live in your area but aren't aware of your business—and lets them know they can find your car wash close by the next time they need one. Second, if some of the people receiving the mailing normally visit another wash, a coupon from you might be just the thing that makes them change their buying habits and visit your wash instead. You should check with your local chamber of commerce or other business owners for recommendations on coupon companies that have had success serving your area.

The second type of direct mail is going to require quite a bit more work on your part. This involves renting or buying mailing lists that you use on your own to contact potential customers in your area. For this to be effective, you should already have a good idea of some criteria you would like recipients of your mail to meet. For instance, perhaps you'd like to reach all registered owners of vehicles in a particular zip code who rent, rather than own their own home. Maybe you'd like to reach those people who have purchased a new car within the past six months or people who fall into a particular income bracket. Whatever the criteria, start to develop some general

---

Theme Schemes

With all the discussion we've had about how to set your car wash apart and attract customers, there's one thing we haven't talked about yet, and that's a theme wash. This is certainly the ultimate in creating a unique setting. Theme washes can take many forms, and depending on how extensively you want to outfit your site, it can get very expensive. Some theme washes can easily run well over $2 million to build.

If you're really into creating a theme wash, there are cheaper alternatives. Some owners have tried creating haunted car washes. These outfits essentially combine the experience of a haunted house with the car wash service. You're most likely going to need some sort of tunnel to make this work, since haunted houses by nature need to be dark.

The equipment you would need for a haunted car wash isn't really that extensive or expensive. A few strobe lights, maybe a fog machine, and some employees to volunteer to put on a monster show for customers. It might be something to think about during the Halloween season to draw in additional customers. Owners who have tried it say that customers generally get a kick out of it, and parents especially enjoy bringing children for the experience.

guidelines for just what type of customer you'll be trying to reach before you move on to the next step.

The next thing you're going to want to do is to find a good mailing-list broker. You can search on the Internet, look in the Yellow Pages, or contact a group such as The Direct Marketing Association (www.thedma.org), which should be able to provide you with some leads.

A good broker is crucial to your success in any direct-mail effort, so spend some time evaluating your options before deciding with which one to work. Direct mail isn't cheap, so it's important that you get the most bang for your buck. You'll probably pay anywhere from $20 to $100 for 1,000 names on a list, depending how targeted the list is, who's offering it, and the format in which it's delivered (the price generally goes up if you get the list on mail-ready labels). Check out www.listsnow.com on the Internet to get a general idea of what's available and what it will cost.

What are some of the services that a good broker will be able to provide? For starters, one will be able to narrow your universe of names and addresses down to only those specific types of people you've identified as being good targets for a direct-mail campaign. For example, corporate CEOs probably aren't the best targets for coupons to a self-service car wash. If you're mailing to the wrong types of people, you're simply wasting money. Second, a good broker will be able to work with you to come up with ideas you may not have thought of before. In other words, you're going to have a general idea of who you want to reach, but the specifics of how to achieve that level of targeting may best be left to the true professionals.

In addition to brokers, there are other sources of mailing lists you may want to consider. Think about where your customers, or potential customers, might "cross over" with other businesses in your area and see if you can strike a deal to obtain their mailing list. It certainly can't hurt to ask. For example, it may be possible to rent or buy mailing lists from local car dealerships, with names and addresses of people who have purchased a new or used car in the past month. You may pay a bit more for a contact by going this route, rather than through a list broker, but it might be worth it for such a highly targeted list.

Another thing to consider when you're marketing through direct mail is that it might be a smart idea to be a bit creative about your offerings. For example, instead of simply providing a

Smart Tip

Tip...

Having trouble thinking about new ways to build business at your wash? Try visiting your competitors as a customer to see if they're doing anything new or innovative.

blanket coupon that covers all times and days of the week, perhaps you may want to offer a midweek special or a similar offer that draws people to your wash during your slower periods.

Door-to-Door Marketing

This type of marketing requires a bit more legwork, but it can be a lot cheaper than paying to obtain mailing lists. No matter where you live, you probably receive fliers under the windshield wipers of your car, on your doorknob at home, or in your mailbox. They tout everything from a home contractor to a new pizzeria. Why not put that method to use for your car wash?

You can try this in a number of different ways. For instance, if there's a local mall or some other location where a large number of cars park, you can try placing fliers on cars, offering discounted washes for one day only, for a week, or whatever you decide. You can also try leaving a stack in the lobby of a large apartment building near your business. Wherever there are people with cars—especially if they don't have adequate space or resources to wash them on their own—there's an opportunity for you to grow your business. Take advantage of it.

One of the drawbacks to this technique is that someone, and it probably isn't going to be you, has to go out and physically distribute the fliers. If you're the trusting sort, you might be comfortable simply handing a stack of fliers to one of your employees and assuming that they'll do the job correctly. However, if you think you might need

---

In the Know

Let's imagine this scenario. You just purchased a four-bay, self-service wash that has been in the community for years. You decide to convert one of the self-service bays into an in-bay automatic unit, but after a few weeks, you're disappointed to find that the automatic unit isn't bringing in the kind of business you had hoped. What's the problem? It could be that your customers don't know it's there.

The solution? Make sure your customers know about all your facilities. Paint arrows on your lot directing them to the automatic bay. Put signs in and around your bays advertising all the choices you're offering. Do this with any detailing services you may offer as well. Put signs in your bays that let people know where your vacuuming islands are, for example. It's a small expense that can make a big difference in your bottom line.

to add a little extra incentive, there are some simple ways to do just that. What about letting your employee know that for every customer who comes in with one of those fliers, the employee will receive a certain percentage of the sale or a flat rate for each car. It doesn't have to be much, just enough to keep them from walking a block or two down the street, dumping the fliers in a garbage can, and taking the rest of the day off. If you make it lucrative enough, you might just find that your employees will jump at the chance to be the "man on the street," rather than viewing it as a chore they'd rather push off on someone else.

Database Marketing

This is probably the most complicated of all the marketing topics we've discussed thus far. It requires ongoing work on your part, as well as some knowledge of computers, to be done right. If you're going to be putting a significant amount of effort into the project, you're going to want a significant return—and according to many car wash experts, you'll get it.

So how does it work? Basically, database marketing is used to track individual customers or groups of customers, allowing you to monitor what they buy and when they buy it. What you'll need is a computer and any one of a number of software packages, such as Microsoft's Access (about $350), that allow you to create a database. The next thing you'll need is some system for recording data in the database; you or one of your employees can do this. The key here is to be as accurate and specific as possible. You want more than just a name for each customer. Ideally, you'd like a name, mailing address, the type of car they drive, and the package they order each time they visit your wash. There may be other pieces of information you'd like to know, but this is pretty much the minimum of what you'll need to make database marketing worthwhile.

It's all well and good to say that's the information you want to collect. But how do you go about collecting it? This is a total team effort. Someone is going to have to record the information initially and then pass it along to the person who will be doing the actual data entry. Who collects this information is up to you; perhaps it will be your cashier or your service writer.

To capture names and contact information initially, it might be a good idea to use one of the other marketing tactics we'll discuss—such as a frequent-buyer program—to get customers to give you that information initially. You can also

Stat Fact
Nearly 45 percent of Americans wash their cars at home most of the time. This gives the car wash industry tremendous room to grow its customer base in the coming years, says the International Carwash Association.

Smart Tip

Tip...

Marketing isn't a one-size-fits-all science. Some approaches may work best with one group (advertising in supermarkets for stay-at-home moms, for example), but not with others. When deciding on the best methods to reach new customers, you should think about who you're trying to attract, based on your community's demographics and the services you provide.

try running some sort of contest or raffle, where customers fill out a card with their name and address, or simply drop off their business card. Maybe you could give away one free deluxe wash or even a coupon book good for several washes if you want to increase the chances that people will take the time to give you their information.

Once you've gathered this information, you can use it in several ways. First, like an auto mechanic might do, you can use the information to determine when a regular customer might be due for a certain type of service—the same way the mechanic might contact a customer when it's time for an oil change. Dropping a quick postcard in the mail costs you virtually nothing, and if it can increase the frequency at which your customers come in, it can be well worth it.

Second, you can get a sense of what types of customers buy what types of wash packages. You can use this information to try to convert a habitual exterior-only customer into a full-service customer. For example, say you notice that you have 500 regular customers who come in once a month for an exterior wash and have never opted for your deluxe package. What do you think would happen if you sent each of those customers a coupon for a free upgrade to a deluxe wash when they purchase their standard exterior-only package? The first result, which is almost definite, is that it will build customer loyalty. After all, you know them well enough to anticipate their car washing needs even before they do. But more important, what might also wind up happening is that the customer sees what a terrific deal the deluxe wash is and becomes a regular deluxe wash buyer. It's almost like saying to the customer "Let me show you what a really great wash makes your car look like. If you don't think it's worth it, then by all means we'd still love to serve you with our standard service." What you're doing is introducing them to something they've never tried before in the hopes that they'll become hooked.

Database marketing can also help you if you decide to embark on a direct-mail campaign that will require you to rent lists. By studying your own customer data, you'll probably be able to spot trends or buying patterns among similar groups of people. Using this information, you can assume that others (who aren't your customers) who share those characteristics might tend to buy the same type of product or service. Then, when you start combing through the mailing lists available, or working with a broker, you can be a bit more specific in terms of the characteristics you're looking for in the list. As we said earlier, direct mail isn't cheap, so any way you can find to increase your rate of response is going to be a big help.

Getting the Word Out

Even before you start accepting customers, there are some things you can do to promote your business. For example, if you're building a new facility, it certainly can't hurt to construct signage, even if it's only temporary, to let passersby know what's coming. People are always curious when they see a construction project underway. How many times have you driven by a building as it's going up and wondered what new business was relocating to your area? Making your presence known even before you're open for business is a great way to get a head start. Put up a sign and let people—especially the drivers who may pass by your wash every day on their way to or from work—get used to seeing it.

If you're buying an existing wash, you might try putting up a sign to let customers know it's under new management. Depending on what the previous owner is comfortable with, he or she might allow you to get a head start on the public relations front by letting you greet customers before you actually take ownership of the location. This might be a good opportunity to meet and greet loyal customers and introduce yourself. You might also get a head start by passing out coupons for a free or reduced-price wash that takes effect after ownership transfers to you.

The real fun starts on the first day you open your doors. That's when you'll get to see all the preparations you've made put to the test. That very first day is going to be your grand opening. And some car wash owners say it's one of the most important times for attracting customers.

Exterior Signage

Your best marketing tool just may be your signage. To understand why, think of it this way: A car wash is something of a unique business. In some ways, it's like the impulse racks at supermarket checkouts. Some of your customers will simply pull into your wash on an impulse. Other customers will have planned to come. It's those impulse customers, the ones who don't have a regular schedule for when they wash their cars, that you want to attract. They may realize that their car needs a wash for a week, two weeks, or even months before they ever get it done. If they happen to be out, have some free time and spot a wash, they'll pull in. These are the customers you need to reach with your signs. Your business will most likely depend on it.

What makes a good sign? Let's talk about your main sign first—the one that's designed to be seen from the street while motorists drive by at whatever rate of speed is typical for your location. First, it must be tall enough to be seen. Second, it must be big enough to be seen. Third, it must be eye-catching enough to be seen. If it's not seen, it's a waste of your money. Keep in mind, that to some degree, your signage choices may be limited by local zoning regulations that you'll have to work within.

Nevertheless, in terms of what goes on the sign itself, there's really only one major rule that nearly every owner agrees on. The words "car wash" need to be the biggest thing on the sign. If you want to decorate it with bubbles or soapsuds, fine. A picture of a shiny, freshly washed and waxed sports car? Great. As long as the words "car wash" are the first and most prominent thing a driver sees, you're in business.

Interior Signage

By interior signage, what we're really talking about are the signs that your customers see once they pull into your property. Of the variety of signs you'll probably have posted, perhaps the most important is your menu of services. This is your bill of fare, the choices, or various levels of service you're offering to your customers. Why is this so

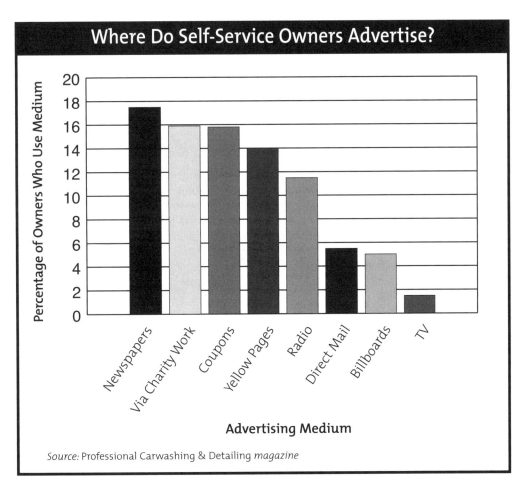

Where Do Self-Service Owners Advertise?

Source: Professional Carwashing & Detailing *magazine*

Let the Truth Be Known

There are many things about car washes your customers probably believe that will tend to keep them away from your business. How much do you think it would cost to print a few hundred fliers that make the true facts known? If you're doing it from your own computer and your own printer, it'll cost next to nothing. Let's examine a few of the harmful myths that you'll probably have to contend with.

○ *Car washes hurt the environment.* It's easy to understand how this myth got started. Take a trip through any car wash tunnel and what do you see? Torrents of water. Not only that, but all the water that's being used is presumably directed to the sewer system—sludge, grease, dirt, and all. Certainly, this can't be good for the environment. That's what most customers probably think, but it's not true.

Many car washes use a water reclamation system that recycles a great deal of the water used in the wash process. Some of these systems can reclaim close to 100 percent of the water used, saving fresh water for rinse cycles only. And there's more: The high-pressure wash systems at professional car washes are designed to do more with less. In other words, they can do a better job at cleaning cars with less water than anything you could do at home. When the typical home washer cleans his car in the driveway, he's using anywhere from 80 to 140 gallons of water every ten minutes. At a professional car wash, a typical wash-and-rinse cycle uses between 8 and 45 gallons, depending on the type of equipment used.

Consider posting a sign that encapsulates this information so that all your customers see it when they enter your wash. Boast about your equipment. Let people know that your water is reclaimed. Position yourself as an environmentally friendly car wash.

○ *Car washes don't get cars clean enough.* No doubt in your own experience with car washes, you've gotten both good and bad washes—that's just the nature of the service. Over the years, as equipment and technology have improved, the effectiveness of car washing equipment has gotten much better. Generally, customers are dissatisfied with the quality of a wash at a place that doesn't specialize in washing cars—such as a gas station. So what you have to do is to point out that your specialty is washing cars. For instance, a local Dodge car dealership in the Philadelphia area uses the slogan: "All we do is discount Dodges." You could say something similar, even being as simple as: "All we do is wash cars."

○ *Car washes damage cars.* This sentiment has probably been around for as long as there have been car washes. Some people feel that it's just too risky to run their car through a commercial wash. They fear all kinds of things—radio antennas or side mirrors being ripped off, or perhaps their paint being scratched by abrasive equipment. In actuality, especially with today's modern touchless equipment, there's a better chance that a customer will scratch or otherwise damage his car if he washes it himself. And again, you can point this out.

Even a simple brochure that you hand out to customers with your menu of services can address these common misconceptions.

important? Think about a restaurant. You want choices. You want choices in terms of the variety of food, and you want choices in terms of price. Car wash customers are not going to be any different. If they want a full-service wash, wax, vacuum, etc., they want to have it available to them. If, on the other hand, they only want a simple and quick exterior cleaning, they aren't going to want to be forced into paying more for services they don't want or feel they need.

While this level of choice isn't going to apply (at least to the same extent) for a self-service wash, for most other types of washes, chances are you're going to be offering numerous levels of service. Your menu of services plays a vital role in marketing your car wash.

Product Sales and Placement

If you choose to sell other products, either in a separate gift shop or in vending machines located in your wash bays or somewhere else on your property, you'll want to think about where the best place is to position whatever it is you're going to be selling. If you're selling from a separate gift store, the location will probably be determined by where you have space for the facility. For vending machines, it's a little bit different. You're probably going to have a much wider range of options. If you have vacuuming facilities, this might not be a bad place to locate your vending machines. Near a change machine is another good option, since you don't want customers to have to search for a place to spend their money once they have it in their hands. Either of these locations will make it easy for your customers to make an impulse buy with any extra change they have left over once they're done with their wash.

If you're operating a tunnel wash, it's not a bad idea to have some vending machines and other products in the customer waiting room, assuming of course that the customers actually leave their car during the wash process. If the customers do stay in the car, you'll probably want to locate the machines in an area where customers are likely to get out of their cars, such as a vacuum island.

Media Advertising

The high cost of advertising on radio and TV probably puts these avenues out of reach for most new car wash owners, unless you can strike a deal with a local cable channel, for example. But there are other media outlets that you might want to explore. Newspapers can be a good place to try, especially local weeklies because the cost is usually much lower than with the major daily papers. An added bonus is that local papers are often much more receptive to giving you actual news coverage if you happen to be a regular advertiser.

You can also try finding newsletters or other publications that cater to a local audience. Is there a large apartment community nearby? Chances are they publish a newsletter that is distributed to residents, probably once a month. These are your prime customers—those without the space or resources to wash their own cars—so tapping into publications such as these can be a great idea. Your best bet is to contact apartment managers in your area to see if such publications exist and whether or not they accept advertising.

Word-of-Mouth Advertising

While all the techniques we've discussed so far can be helpful, there's also a form of advertising that you can't buy—at least not directly. Word-of-mouth advertising is very important to a neighborhood business such as a car wash. Nothing beats one neighbor telling another that a new restaurant, new store, or new car wash is a great place to take your business.

Traditional advertising that you pay for can help bring customers to your shop initially, but once they get there, you have to continue to deliver—through quality services, friendly employees, and fair prices—so that they, in turn, will turn into advertisers for you.

Special Promotions

Many, many companies use what are called premiums to attract or retain customers. America Online, the Internet giant, once gave away books as part of a retention premium—a gift designed to encourage customers to renew their subscription to the service. The gift was a book that retailed for about $10. In truth, America Online probably bought the books for around $3 or $4 each. It's a simple equation. If you spend $3 to keep a customer who's going to wind up spending at least $200 over the course of the year, isn't that worth it? How might you follow America Online's example at your car wash?

Premium Deals

Consider which companies or organizations out there would like to give away books of coupons for free car washes to their members or customers. There are

Stat Fact

Nearly 50 percent of self-service owners don't advertise at all, according to a recent survey by *Professional Carwashing & Detailing* magazine. Lower prices (and thus lower revenue from each customer) probably make it cost-prohibitive.

probably dozens of them. Some might include local car clubs, new or used car dealerships, churches, and a host of charitable organizations.

Bear in mind that you aren't giving away anything. The way a premium deal works is that the company or organization buys the coupon books from you, and they in turn give them away to their members or customers. The best part, depending on how you look at it, is that this is money that you're going to make whether or not the final recipient of the coupons ever uses them or not. In other words, you may make money for washing cars that you may never actually wash. It doesn't get much better than that.

So, how should you go about approaching these organizations? The first message you must convey is that your coupon books will provide some sort of value to the eventual recipient. For example, have you ever heard ads for car dealerships that offer $100 worth of free gas with any new or used car purchase? They're doing it simply because it's an added incentive for a customer to make a purchase from that dealership, rather than from one down the road offering a similar price on a similar car. This can work the same way with a book of 10 or 20 coupons for a free car wash. The dealerships buy the books from you, and then offer them as an added bonus when salespeople are trying to close the deal.

The same holds true for other organizations. Banks, for example, are famous for giving away items such as calendars every year. But while many people probably just throw out a calendar, there's a much greater chance that they'll hold onto a book full of coupons for a free car wash, since this represents a real value. This is the message you want to get across to whatever organization you approach: The gift is going to mean something.

The second point you want to stress is that the customer will remember and associate the gift with the company or organization that gave it to them. Help them along with this by offering to customize the product. You might offer free customization to any "bulk buyer" who purchases more than 100 coupon books, for example. All you have to do is print the company's name (or some other message of their choosing) alongside your own in the coupon book. You might also want to try offering discounts to companies that buy a large quantity.

One-Day-Only Specials

One of the central tenets of marketing is that you should give people who might not otherwise buy your product or service a reason to buy. Movie theaters do this

Stat Fact
According to a recent survey by *Professional Carwashing & Detailing* magazine, nearly three out of four car wash owners use coupons as a way of providing discounts.

when they offer senior-citizen discounts. Part of it may be goodwill, but you can bet the real reason they do it is because they've discovered that, by reducing the price, more seniors are inclined to come to the movies.

If you anticipate that traffic is going to be particularly slow on a certain day, you might try jazzing it up a bit by running a one-day-only special—maybe a discounted wash or a free add-on service. You can also try running midweek specials. Many establishments, such as dry cleaners, run specials on clothes brought in during the week, as opposed to those dropped off on a Saturday or Sunday. Since the weekend is most likely going to be your busiest time, try reducing your price slightly or adding services for those days of the week when you notice that your traffic flow slacks a bit. The beauty of this type of promotion is that it adds a sense of urgency. A driver on the fence, wavering between getting his car washed and waiting another couple of weeks, might just decide now is the time if he really wants to take advantage of the special you're running. As mentioned above, Mike G. from Carson City, California, uses midweek specials on his slowest days to attract more customers.

Holiday specials are another option and can be anything you want them to be. Run a Mother's Day special, where moms get a reduced-price wash. Run a Halloween special, where every customer with children gets a piece of candy.

If customers come to expect these types of promotions, it can also help to build a base of regulars who choose your wash over another because they know they're always going to get a better value from you. Today it might be a free wax application, tomorrow it might be a free vacuum; it doesn't matter. Whatever it is, it's more than what the guy down the street is offering.

Frequent-Buyer Programs

In the car wash business, loyalty is very important. Since the services you're going to provide will be very similar to the competition, you're going to need to find a way to differentiate yourself. A frequent-buyer promotion might be just the ticket.

You've probably seen these types of promotions in a variety of different businesses. Coffee shops, bakeries, and lunch counters in

Tip...

Smart Tip
Build customer loyalty by being around your wash as much as possible and making a point to remember your frequent customers. If you own a self-service wash, every third or fourth wash, give them a free wash to say thanks. Almost nothing makes customers feel better than to know the owner appreciates their business.

areas frequented by business people often use them. Just in case you aren't familiar with how these programs work, here's what happens. Each customer who comes into the store receives a business-card-sized coupon. This coupon will typically have ten or more squares around its perimeter. Each time the customer returns and makes a purchase, the cashier punches out one of the squares or marks it with a special stamp. When all the squares are gone or marked, the customer receives a free coffee, or a loaf of bread, or a discounted lunch—whatever the store happens to sell.

You can do exactly the same thing with your car wash. You can use it in a number of different ways, too. You might want to make the freebie an upgrade from a standard to a deluxe wash. Or you might simply want to offer a free standard wash. Experience will tell you what works best for your car wash.

Cross-Merchandising

Let's say your wash is located a block away from a gas station or convenience store. Assuming these establishments aren't offering, and don't plan to offer, car washing services, they represent a prime target for a cross-merchandising opportunity. Your goal here is to use their store or station to drive customers to your wash. This can be accomplished in a number of ways. The most popular is to have the store give their customers coupons for a discounted wash (perhaps $1 or $2 off the regular wash price) when they buy a certain amount of goods.

It may seem odd at first for an unrelated store to help you promote your business for free. After all, it's not like you're going to be offering $1 off a gas purchase with the purchase of a deluxe wash. But when you think about it, you begin to see that the store is getting something out of the arrangement as well. If the offer is for a discounted wash when the customer buys a certain amount—$10 worth of a gas or a fill-up, for example—you're helping the store increase the average purchase from each customer. It wouldn't make sense for the other business not to agree to help you out.

Public Relations

The day the cars start rolling into your wash isn't just important because you'll finally start seeing a return on your investment. It's also important because this is when you get your first, and perhaps best, chance to hype your wash to the hilt.

The Grand Opening

The goal with any grand opening is to create, for lack of a better word, a spectacle. You want people to pay attention. You want drivers to stop. You even want pedestrians to take a look at what's going on (they probably have cars, too). One car wash

Bright Idea

Offer insurance for your customers. No, not health insurance or automotive insurance, but rain insurance. Guarantee that if it rains less than 24 hours after they wash their car, you'll wash it again for free when they show you their receipt. This can help boost business on days when people might hold off getting a wash because of poor weather reports.

consulting company rents a giant inflatable turtle to help draw customers to their clients' grand openings. That's certainly a start. Surely, you're going to want to have flags flapping in the wind. Depending on your location, you might also be able to put employees with signs along the sidewalk (as long as they aren't in danger of being struck by passing cars). The bottom line is that you don't want to rule anything out that you think might work.

In terms of specifically what you can do during your grand opening, it's pretty wide open. To help you think of some ideas, try to remember the last grand opening you attended for a store that you now regularly visit. Think specifically about what attracted you to the location. This may give you some idea of things you can try with your own car wash.

Give a good deal of thought to the timing of your grand opening. Remember the statistics about when most washes do their best business. To generalize, you can probably say that a sunny Saturday morning or an afternoon in the cold winter months are going to be your busiest times. It may seem like this would be a great time for a grand opening. However, think about how much experience you have in the car wash business. It certainly wouldn't be a very auspicious start for your new business if you happened to get "slammed" on your very first day and wound up with slow or inadequate service as a result. It might be better to give yourself a few days to familiarize yourself with the operation, with what goes wrong, with common things you have to deal with to keep things running smoothly, before you try to tackle a really full day.

Remember, your grand opening doesn't have to be on just one day either. It could conceivably last for an entire week, or even an entire month. It might be best for you to open in the middle of the week, get at least a feel for what you can expect, and for some of the issues you're going to have to deal with on a daily basis, and then tackle the weekend crowds.

Let's say you designate the month of February as your grand opening period. During the first week, maybe you can offer half-price washes. During the second week, maybe you can offer a free upgrade to your best wash at the regular wash price. For the third week, maybe you could offer a coupon for a free or discounted wash during the customer's next visit. For the fourth week, perhaps you could offer discounted coupon books good for five or ten washes over a certain period of time. Those are just some suggestions, but you can see how extending the grand opening period allows you to make more of an impact on the car wash customer. Not only will you capture people who don't happen to drive by your wash every day, you'll also give yourself the opportunity to turn those occasional customers into regulars by offering them a reason to come back.

Charity Partnerships

Hosting a car wash is a tried-and-true method for many charities—especially schools, and academically related clubs and teams—to raise money for their cause. Oftentimes, a charity event will be held in a parking lot or similar venue on school grounds, where the kids will normally wash and dry cars using handheld sponges and buckets of soapy water. How do you think the kids would feel about having the use of your car wash for a day? No, you're not going to turn over the keys to the shop. But you can arrange to donate part of your revenue from that day to their cause.

Exactly what formula you use is up to you. Maybe you simply donate a percentage of your revenue, a specific amount for each car washed above what your normal volume would be on that day, or some other arrangement you come up with. Why, you may be asking at this point, does this make sense for you? Sure, the charity benefits, but what does your business get out of it? Well, a lot actually.

The first thing you get out of it is goodwill in your community. While this isn't something you can put a price tag on, you can certainly understand that there's a big difference between being seen as an altruistic business owner instead of a miser. Remember, the vast majority of your customers are going to come from within three or four miles of your location. You are very much tied to the community in which your car wash lies.

Second, you're getting your own personal public relations squad for free. Instead of the band members promoting a car wash they held on their own in some vacant parking lot, they'll now be promoting your car wash. There's no doubt they'll be doing some PR campaigning before the event by encouraging supporters to show up, but you should also ask them to come to your business on the big day to help pull in passersby.

Third, you have a great chance, or at least a much better chance, of getting free publicity for your wash when the charity asks for it, as opposed to when you, as a business owner, ask for it. In summary, charity partnerships can help promote your business by pulling in customers who you wouldn't otherwise get. In addition to those who make a point to show up for a wash, chances are you'll find that others who hadn't planned on getting

> **Bright Idea**
>
> If you really want your customers to remember you, why not give out free key chains with punch-out slots that can be used to track your frequent-washer program?

▲

> **Bright Idea**
>
> If you have a waiting room, offer free coffee or tea to your customers. It doesn't cost you much, and it shows you're doing everything you can to make their experience a pleasant one.

their cars washed that day will take the opportunity to help a cause they believe in.

Customer Relations

As we've mentioned, one of the keys to running a successful car wash business over the long haul is customer service. People simply won't come back if they feel they haven't been treated properly. If you're on-site during the hours of operation, as you most likely will be if you operate any kind of conveyor wash, you'll have ample opportunity to take care of your customers. For owners of self-service washes, this task will be more challenging. They'll have to be a bit more creative in how they gather customer feedback and handle complaints.

As a self-service owner, you're going to have to devise ways to stay in touch with your customers, even though you aren't there at all times. One of the ways that many owners accomplish this is to place phone numbers in a conspicuous area of their wash so that customers will always have someone to contact in the event of a problem. If you don't have an office and don't want customers calling you at home, you should install a business line in your home so that customers can leave messages if you don't happen to be available. You might also consider getting a cellular phone. This could turn out to be cheaper and more effective than having a second line installed in your home.

Regardless of the type of wash you will operate, when you do get a complaint, it's vitally important that you respond right away. Nothing is more frustrating for a customer than to feel that his or her complaint is falling on deaf ears. If someone calls you and says your equipment malfunctioned and that your machine ate their money, send a refund promptly. Some owners go even further and refund the money lost, plus provide a token for a free wash on top of it. What you actually decide to do isn't as important as just making sure that you do something promptly to satisfy the customer.

Measuring Your Success

One of the key components of any marketing plan is that you must know how well it performs for you. If you don't measure the results of your advertising efforts, how will you know if you're spending your money wisely?

Let's take a look at one example of how you might determine what's working and what's not with one of the techniques we've mentioned already—distributing fliers door-to-door.

Let's say that on the day you're handing out the fliers, you would expect 50 cars to order a full-service wash, if you did no additional advertising. Let's also assume that you pay one of your employees $8 an hour to distribute the fliers for you, and that each flier has a $2 off coupon attached for a full-service wash. Finally, let's put the price of your full-service treatment at $10 (without any coupons).

Without distributing the fliers, you would be making $500 (50 cars x $10 a car). Now, let's say that your employee works for three hours distributing the fliers, meaning you're incurring $24 in labor costs. You would need only three cars to come in because of the fliers ($8 discounted wash x 3 cars = $24) to make the effort pay for itself. Anything above that, and you're making more money than you would have if you did nothing at all.

To take it one step further, if you are using database marketing to track your customers, you'd be able to determine who among the people who came in that day had never been to your wash before. As you track them over time, you'll probably find that at least some of them will become regulars. This is when you can truly start to see if the extra effort is worthwhile.

It can be much the same with any other type of marketing effort. The key is to operate your promotion in such a way that you can achieve some sort of measurable result—good or bad. Over time, you'll learn what works best, and what is best left out, of your marketing effort. Like Mike G., the car wash owner in Carson, California, who found, after running lots of different promotional programs, that advertising on the back of supermarket register tapes gave him the most bang for his buck, you'll want to keep track of the estimated gains in business, and compare those to the costs it took to achieve those gains. We've provided a chart on page 142 to help you track your progress.

Measuring Your Marketing Efforts

Here's a chart that can help you track the effectiveness of the various market-ing methods you try. When you see how each performs, you can start to make decisions about which are most effective and which you should drop. The methods listed here are just a few examples. You can create your own chart with additional methods as you try them.

Method	Direct Mail	Newspaper Ads	Fliers	Cross-Merchandising	Discount Coupons
Number of new customers					
Total Revenue	$	$	$	$	$
Revenue from each customer (*total revenue divided by number of customers*)	$	$	$	$	$
Total Cost of Campaign	$	$	$	$	$
Cost for each customer (*total cost divided by number of customers*)	$	$	$	$	$
Profit or Loss	$	$	$	$	$

Long-Term
Considerations

As your business grows, there are going to be a number of decisions you're eventually going to have to make that will determine the future direction of your car wash. As Yogi Berra once advised, "When you come to a fork in the road, you're going to have to take it." Here are some of the decisions you may find yourself faced with as you grow your business.

▲

Expansion Into Other Services or Products

As your business grows, your customer base increases, and you begin to develop a solid reputation in the community, you may start thinking about trying to duplicate the success you've had in washing cars by expanding into other services or products. This is a common practice among car wash owners.

One of the hot trends today is to add quick lube or oil change services. Detailing is another service some owners choose. Whether or not these are right for you really depends on what you're looking to get out of the business. Assuming there's a need for the services you're thinking about offering, and that you can provide what customers want, you're going to be adding another profit center to your business. But with the extra money come extra headaches. You'll have more employees to deal with, the possible expansion of your physical facilities to tackle, and learning the ins and outs of a whole new business (new suppliers to find and evaluate, new equipment to learn about, etc.) to contend with. If you're considering expanding into other areas, it might make sense to start slowly at first. You can always beef up the operation if it turns out to be something you enjoy doing and adds to your bottom line.

In addition to adding offline services—such as quickie lube jobs or oil changes—there's also the possibility that you may want to try to expand your existing business by offering a larger range of wash options. There are any number of different ways in which you can expand. You might convert an existing self-service bay to handle an in-bay automatic unit. Or you may decide to offer the cheaper alternative of an exterior-conveyor wash at your full-service car wash. There are other options of course, but these are some typical ones.

This is probably a somewhat easier task to accomplish than expanding your business into an area with which you're unfamiliar (such as a convenience store). There are definitely some issues to consider if you want to expand into offering products, as opposed to services—as in the case of opening a convenience store on your property. Remember, one of the things that may have initially attracted you to a car wash business is that you essentially don't have inventory to worry about. Sure, you have supplies such as soap and wax, but traditional inventory is something you basically don't have to worry about. It's the exact opposite with a convenience store. Your entire business is your inventory. Think about whether you want to devote the time to handle this. If not, you may want to think twice about the viability of the project. You can also look into hiring a full-time manager who would handle only that part of the business.

The basic thing you'll want to consider, whether you decide to branch out into additional services or products, is whether your local market can support what you want to offer. You'll need to conduct market research, just as you did when you initially bought or built your car wash. If you can demonstrate to yourself that the area can support the new business, you've passed the first test.

When you expand into other services, you're once again going to have to go through the process of drawing new customers to your wash. It's likely your efforts won't have to be as involved as with an entirely new business, but it's going to have to be done just the same. Exactly how much work you're going to have to put into this is going to vary. It will tend to be less if you're offering slight upgrades or downgrades in service—adding an in-bay automatic to an existing self-service wash, for example—and a bit more work if the offerings attract radically different segments of the carwash-buying public.

With that said, expanding into other products and services is still a pretty common practice among established car wash owners. It's an option that you'll probably at least consider at some point down the road.

Opening Satellite Locations

This is where you get to become a car wash mogul. Your initial business has done so well that you can imagine a satellite location basically doubling your revenue. This may very well be the case. The biggest difference, however, is that you'll be locked into becoming an absentee owner at one of your locations, at least part of the time. Because of this, you're going to need an experienced manager who can handle your duties when you're not around. You're probably going to want that manager to oversee operations at your first wash while you concentrate on the new location.

Stat Fact
According to a recent survey by *Professional Carwashing & Detailing* magazine, nearly half of all self-service owners own more than one location.

Depending on how much responsibility you turn over to someone else, keep in mind that running two car washes is twice the work of running one car wash. If you're pushing yourself to the limit in terms of time or energy with your first wash, it doesn't make much sense to think that things will get better by adding even more work. However, if you are able to turn over a large portion of the day-to-day duties to a manager, it might be possible to make things work with only a marginal increase in the effort you have to expend.

Valuing and Selling Your Business

There may come a time when you decide it's time to cash out. After years of building your business, you may start thinking about selling it. When you start the selling

Stat Fact

More than 55 percent of full-service owners (and 51 percent of exterior-conveyor owners) have been approached about selling their businesses, according to a survey in *Professional Carwashing & Detailing* magazine.

process, obviously the first thing you're going to want to do is to figure out how much your business is worth. A good place to start is with an appraiser—someone who will look at your facilities and your books, and determine what your wash is worth. Local banks and lenders who regularly make loans to the business community will probably have someone who can pass sound judgment. It's best to find someone who has experience with businesses similar to your wash, so you should make a few calls until you find someone qualified for the job. Don't stop with just one either. Try to get a few opinions so that you can use the higher number as a basis for your negotiations with potential buyers.

Some other pieces of information that will help you determine a possible selling price are your gross income multiplier (GIM) and net income multiplier (NIM) for similar washes in your area that have sold recently. To figure GIM, divide the selling price of a wash by yearly gross revenue. For example, if a wash sold for $500,000, and it took in $200,000 in revenue, the GIM would be 2.5. The NIM calculation works the same way, just substituting net income for gross revenue. An appraiser can help you with this and then compare these figures with your own. This will help give you an idea of how your wash fits into the overall car wash market in your area.

The eventual selling price will be some multiple of the profits you make every year. Exactly what that multiple will be depends on a number of things including your sales growth rate, the age of your facilities, as well as the GIM and NIM of similar washes in your area.

The timing of your sale is also very important. If you're trying to sell during a period of relatively high interest rates, it's going to be harder for someone to meet the price you're asking. Conversely, during periods of low interest rates, it will be easier for smaller investors to meet their loan payment, while still taking a decent profit out of the business. If you find that the times simply aren't conducive to selling your business, it's probably a good idea to wait a while until the economy becomes more favorable.

What You Need to Succeed

In the long run, your chances for success in the car wash business will depend on a number of factors—some within your control and a few you can't do anything about.

In this section, we'll try to give you some idea of the factors you can control so that you'll be able to maximize your chances for success.

Location, Location, Location

How many times has this topic come up in this guide? Probably more than any other. There's a reason for that. Just about everyone you talk to in the car wash business says location is the number-one factor that will ultimately determine your success or failure. Remember the line from Steve Gaudreau of Power Inc.'s Car Wash Institute? "I've seen bad car washes in good locations succeed, and good car washes in bad locations fail."

Remember to consider not just traffic count, but site visibility, traffic patterns, street position, local government cooperation (or lack thereof), proximity to competitors, access to labor, signage regulations, and potential for expansion. These are all important factors that should play a role in how you decide if a location is viable for your car wash.

Service and Quality

Beyond your location, the other factors that will make or break your business all have to do with how you compete with other car washes in your area. The level of service and quality you provide will be paramount. Remember how we told you that car washes can be a fairly homogenous service? That's true to the extent that people will hardly ever drive very far out of their way to get a better wash, if there's another one that does almost as good a job right down the street.

Nevertheless, you shouldn't assume that just because your area is devoid of a competitor that you can let your service and quality slide. For one thing, poor service and quality mean that your regular customers (and they'll only be regulars because you're the only game in town) will probably visit you less often. If it's bad enough, they may drive those extra couple of miles to your nearest competitor.

The bottom line is that, if you get a reputation for poor service, you're inviting trouble. Word gets around. Your neighbors talk to each other. They know the good businesses in town and the bad ones. Being one of the good ones can only help your cause.

Price

If you have a great location and impeccable service, you can probably get away with charging a bit more than the average for a wash. There's no better example of this than the old competition between the "free with fill up" washes at gas stations and the car wash-only business that charges $5, $10, or more for what appears to be the same service.

Owners who compete with these types of washes say the overriding fear many car wash owners feel when one of these systems goes up near them is unfounded. Sure,

▲

Know When to Hold 'Em

In the long run, being able to attract and retain quality employees will be vital to your success, just as it was for Dick H., the car wash entrepreneur in Sacramento, California. "You can't just manage the money," he says. "You need to have competent people running your wash, and you need to pay them well, especially your manager. This is a tough business, and everyone—your employees, your managers, and your customers—are all part of the components that go into running a successful business."

Mike G., the car wash owner in Carson, California, agrees. Even though he has an MBA and has no problem with balance sheets and cash flow analysis, it's still his employees who keep his business humming. "My service writer is probably the most important person I've got," he says. And that's probably the reason his service writer makes more money than anyone else at his wash.

some people may take advantage of the free wash once. But after they see what a generally poor job these washes do, they'll be back to you for a real car wash, even though they have to pay more for it.

So you don't have to necessarily be the cheapest kid on the block. But, and this is a big but, you do have to remain reasonably close to what others are charging. Let's face it, there's no car wash for which people are willing to pay a Rolls Royce price. If two washes both clean cars reasonably well, both have about the same quality of service, and the locations are equally accessible, the one with the lower price is going to do better. It's just that's simple.

Mechanical Skill

We've been saying throughout this book that running a car wash is not a job for a desk jockey. Yes, there's some paperwork involved (perhaps quite a bit depending on what type of wash you have), but if it's a cushy office chair you're looking for, you're better off becoming an accountant.

Your business relies on a long list of equipment to run smoothly. And as we all know, anything with moving parts is going to break down sooner or later. When it does break down, your ability to get it up and running again—and quickly—is going to mean the difference between staying in business and shutting down temporarily.

We're not talking about major malfunctions here. Those are most likely going to be handled by the person who sold you the equipment. Rather, we're talking about the minor glitches that can occur on any given day—a malfunctioning weep system that causes your wands to freeze in extremely cold weather, a jammed change machine, a cracked nozzle. If you're someone who can't fathom the thought of changing the oil in your car or fixing a broken pipe, you're going to have a difficult time in the car wash business, unless you have someone on-call 24 hours a day to do these kinds of things for you. And even that's not as reliable an option as being able to do some repairs yourself.

Business Acumen

This is the other side of the coin. With any business, not just a car wash business, your ability to work with numbers, develop a business plan and market it effectively, compete with other businesses, and generally run the show like a professional is going to be one of the factors that determines your success or failure.

So what do you need to know? Well, we're certainly not going to tell you that you have to go back to school and get an MBA. But it does help if you have some general knowledge of how to make a budget, calculate cash flow and revenue projections, determine your level of profitability and return on investment, and just generally make sense of all the numbers you're going to deal with every day.

Unless you pay cash for your wash, the money you pay back to the bank every month for your loan will be something with which you have to contend, too. Paying back this loan is inevitably going to come before other things you may want to do—like adding an automatic bay to a self-service wash. If you had plans to expand or modernize when you bought an existing wash, you'll need to be able to assess whether it's practical to do so and still meet your financial obligations to your creditors.

You're going to need to be able to determine where your greatest revenue-generating areas are and how to maximize the revenue you get from each car. You should also be able to identify where you may be losing money, and either cut costs or increase revenues to make that area profitable (or eliminate it from your services altogether). If you aren't good at keeping and analyzing records, it will be that much harder for you to operate your business at its maximum potential.

Reliable Suppliers

Time and time again we hear the same thing from car wash owners: "It's the suppliers, stupid." Or, to be more exact, the distributors. Many first-time car wash owners are overly concerned with the type of equipment they buy and the manufacturer who makes it, instead of focusing on the people who can really help you grow your business—local distributors.

The choice of distributors that you make at the outset of your business, as well as how well you keep up your relationship with your distributors over the course of time, is going to play a large factor in your business' success. What you're looking for are distributors with a great record of service. You can ask other owners in your area (unless they're a direct competitor of yours, you'll probably get an honest answer) who the top-notch distributors are, and then work to build the best relationship you possibly can with them.

Dedicated Employees

We've spent lots of time in this book talking about employees, and rightly so. No man is an island, and that goes for car wash owners, too. Unless you have a single-bay, self-service wash, you're going to need employees to help you run it. We can't stress enough how the quality of those employees is going to affect your bottom line. While you can think of yourself as the commander of your wash, you're going to need quality front-line troops to be successful.

Over the long term, the kind of employees you have will depend on how successful you are at developing your personnel strategy. How well can you integrate your training program with the overall philosophy of your wash? How well can you manage to retain the top employees you have, and get rid of those who don't measure up? How will you compensate your employees to keep them from leaving for greener pastures elsewhere, and how will you replace the ones who do leave?

Ask around and most car wash owners will tell you that a good employee is a tremendously valuable asset. They'll pay them what they have to, and maybe even a little bit more, in order not to lose them. You would be smart to think long and hard about how you plan to make your employees one of your wash's best assets.

Repeat Customers

How proficient you are at keeping the customers who visit your wash coming back will be, over the long haul, one of the most important indicators of whether your business will succeed or fail. The reason, as we've mentioned, is the incredible cost of attracting new customers.

Remember Mike G., the car wash owner from Carson, California? He's been in the business for six years and never runs advertising. Yet he has a steady flow of cars into his wash every day. Why? Because he's been able to build a base of customers who know and trust his work. When he first bought his business, he did advertise. But because he was so good at retaining those initial customers that he did attract through advertising, he no longer has to expend advertising dollars to draw new ones. If you've created a strong presence in the community and if people have come to associate your car wash with quality service, word will get around. This is the real key to constantly refreshing your customer base—and it's a heck of a lot cheaper than advertising and discounts.

This doesn't mean that after five years in the business you're going to be seeing the same cars over and over again. You'll get new customers, and with any luck those will

Keep Them Coming Back

You'd expect happy customers to return to your car wash, and most likely they will. But no matter how hard you try, there are going to be customers that aren't completely satisfied with the service they receive. How do you turn them around? What's the secret to bringing even dissatisfied customers back to your wash?

The key is not to treat customer complaints as a battle—as a struggle to prove who's right and who's wrong. Instead, if you treat it as a joint effort to find the source of the problem and then to solve it, you'll have a much better chance at winning over all but the most unyielding customers. Steve Gaudreau of Power Inc.'s Car Wash Institute says that it's possible to get as many as 70 percent of your initially dissatisfied customers back, if you handle the situation properly.

become regulars. It also doesn't mean that you'll never want to expand and attract a larger client base, but the core of your business is most likely going to come from repeat customers.

Tales from the Trenches

We're going to share some of the experiences of the entrepreneurs interviewed for this book so that you can benefit from their hard-won wisdom and guard against the unforeseen pitfalls that strike just about any business from time to time.

Richard K., owner of a ten-bay self-service/in-bay automatic combo outside of Chicago, advises equipping your wash to give yourself a chance to expand your business later on. He says one of the big mistakes he made was not building a pump room large enough to handle the increased water requirements of a number of automatics. It may cost a bit more in the beginning, but it can increase the value of your wash, plus give you more options down the road.

Dick H., the full-service owner in Sacramento, California, who's been in the business since 1975, stresses getting some car wash industry experience—before you buy. He sold car wash products for five years before he bought his own shop. Dick says, "It gave me a lot better feel for the business because we had to pick out and evaluate sites."

According to Mike G., you don't necessarily have to increase the number of customers you serve to be successful. Mike says his volume is actually down 10 percent from the previous owner, but that total sales are up. Why? He changed some procedures (by adding more extensive wash packages) that slowed down the line but increased the average revenue he makes from each car.

If you're going to succeed in the long run, you need to keep on top of changes or new services that your customers are looking for. That's one reason they can be some of your best sources of new ideas for how to improve your wash. Dick says he routinely gets new ideas by talking to his customers, including the realization that the

---

Beyond Your Control

Your success in the car wash business will depend on a number of factors. Some of these will be things you can control, and some will be largely beyond your control. What factors are likely to be out of your control? Take a look at the ones we've listed below.

○ *The weather.* You do have control over where in the country you decide to open your wash. But it's probably highly unlikely that you're going to move halfway across the country just to open your new business. During the first few months of operation, as your business is in its all-important incubation phase, you might have terrible luck and have one rainy weekend after another, seriously putting a damper, not only on your mood but on your profits.

Over the long run, however, the weather is going to balance out. Over the course of several years, you're pretty much going to get whatever weather is average for your section of the country.

○ *New competition.* If a gas station wants to install an automatic rollover across the street from your wash, there's not much you can do about it. Nor can you do much about the full-service wash down the street installing self-service bays to compete with your own. The best you can do is to open your wash, or buy an existing wash, in an area that is incredibly underserved by car washes.

One of the best ways to discourage unexpected competition is by running one hell of a car wash. If a competitor comes snooping around your territory, let him see the great job you're doing—the well-kept wash with courteous and knowledgeable employees. Who would want to open a new business to compete against a guy already doing it the best way it can be done?

○ *The economy.* Self-service washes seem to suffer in a poor economy, as do exterior-conveyor and full-service washes, and just about every other type of business. If you're unlucky enough to start your business at the outset of, say, a recession, it might be difficult to turn any kind of meaningful profit until the economy picks up again.

time they were willing to wait for service had shrunk dramatically in recent years. If he hadn't gotten that feedback from his customers, he almost certainly would have lost business.

No matter how thoroughly you plan your new business, there are going to be surprises. If you painted too rosy a picture for yourself during the planning phase, these surprises can come back to haunt you later on and could jeopardize your chances for

---

Beyond Your Control, continued

○ *New regulations.* What was once a car wash-friendly business environment could turn decidedly sour overnight with unexpected regulation changes. Talking to zoning boards in your area can be helpful in order to get a feel for what the regulatory environment is likely to be like later on down the road. But unfortunately, you just never know what politicians will do in response to, say, a shooting or a string of muggings at an area self-service wash. You might also face changes in environmental regulations or some other shift in policy that causes you to install costly new equipment or otherwise drastically change the process of washing cars. It can't hurt to keep your eyes and ears open for rumblings that could signify these kinds of changes. You should also consider lobbying your local officials in the event of a regulation change that will be particularly costly to your business.

○ *Utility rate increases.* Utilities are going to be a major expense for any car wash owner, and there's very little you can do about it. The only way to use less water, for example, is to wash fewer cars—and that would amount to cutting off your nose to spite your face. The only remedy (besides making sure you start out with energy-efficient equipment, for example) is to raise prices or be satisfied with whatever reduced profit you can make after a rate hike. The only saving grace is that other washes in your area will most likely be faced with the same dilemma, so it isn't like you'll be competing on unequal footing.

○ *Water shortages.* When areas of the country experience drought conditions, some of the first businesses affected are usually car washes. Unfortunately, the perception is that car washes are terrible water-wasters. As we've pointed out, this simply isn't true. Other than educating those in charge, by providing them with the actual statistics that show how water-friendly car washes are, there's really nothing you can do if your locality decides to shut you down for a period of time. As you might imagine, this can be devastating. If you do happen to find yourself in this situation, you had better hope you have enough cash put away to ride it out.

153

▲

long-term success. For example, Mike G. said he was very surprised that the improvements he planned to make upon buying his site took a lot longer to finish than he initially thought. Luckily, it didn't affect his income. But if you were in the same situation, and you were counting on those improvements to increase your customer base and drive up revenue, you might find yourself in a disastrous situation.

How can smart cash flow play a role in the long-term success of your wash? During his 17 years in the self-service business, Richard K. says one of the most important changes in the industry has been "the huge influx of in-bay automatics." Since it costs at least two or three times as much to equip an automatic bay as it does a self-service bay, if you lacked the capital to modernize, you'd be left behind. "Twenty years ago, almost all self-serves were built exclusively as self-serves," he says. "Now just about everyone has an automatic. They've been the survival of the self-serve business." How do you think you'd manage if you lacked the funds to keep up with Joneses?

The Bottom Line

We began this book by trying to dispel some of the myths you probably believed about the car wash business, and now might be a good time to go back and reiterate one of the more important points. This is not a business that you can run on autopilot. That should be obvious after having gone through all of the material in this guide. You can't simply put down your money, walk away, and watch the profits roll in. But what should also be obvious is that, for as long as people drive cars, they're going to need to get them washed. If you can provide that service with a level of quality, for a fair price, and in a reasonable amount of time, you'll be well on the way to success. And on a final note, make sure you take the time to research your chosen industry and properly equip yourself with the tools you'll need to make your new car wash a success. Good luck!

Appendix
Car Wash Resources

They say you can never be rich enough or young enough. While these could be argued, we believe you can never have enough resources. Therefore, we present for your consideration a wealth of sources for you to check into, check out, and harness for your own personal information blitz.

These sources are tidbits, ideas to get you started on your research. They are by no means the only sources out there, and they should not be taken as the Ultimate Answer. We have done our research, but businesses do tend to move, change, fold, and expand. As we have repeatedly stressed, do your homework. Get out and start investigating.

As an additional tidbit to get you going, we strongly suggest the following: If you haven't yet joined the Internet Age, do it! Surfing the Net is like waltzing through a vast library, with a breathtaking array of resources literally at your fingertips.

Associations

Car Wash Operators of New Jersey (CWONJ), P.O. Box 48, Maywood, NJ 07607, e-mail: www.cwonj1@aol.com, www.cwonj.com

Chicagoland Carwash Association, P.O. Box 298, Lockport, IL 60441, (708) 301-3568

▲

Connecticut Carwash Association, P.O. Box 28, Clifton Park, NY 12065, (518) 877-6779, e-mail: mediasolxx@aol.com, www.ct-carwash.org

Greater St. Louis Professional Car Wash Association, 1700 Ford Ln., St. Charles, MO 63303, (314) 949-5000

Heartland Carwash Association, Iowa Membership Area, P.O. Box 932, Des Moines, IA 50304, (515) 965-3190, fax: (515) 965-3191

International Carwash Association, 401 N. Michigan Ave., Chicago, IL 60611-4267, (312) 321-5199, fax: (312) 245-1085, e-mail: ica@sba.com, www.carwash.org

Ohio Car Wash Association, P.O. Box 9224, Canton, OH 44711, (303) 492-8761

Southeastern Carwash Association, P.O. Box 330, Pelham, AL 35124, (205) 991-3552, fax: 205-991-6771, e-mail: secwa@secwa.com, www.secwa.com

Southwest Car Association, 4600 Spicewood Springs Rd., #103, Austin, TX 78759, (512) 349-9023, fax: (512) 343-1530, e-mail: info@swcarwash.org, www.swcarwash.org

Western Carwash Association, 10535 Paramount Blvd., #100, Downey, CA 90241, (562) 928-6928, fax: (562) 928-9557, e-mail: wcarwa@aol.com, www.wcwa.org

Consultants

Power Inc.'s Car Wash Institute, 30 Church St., Salem, MA 01970, (800) 633-9003, www.powercarwash.com

Note: Most of the major manufacturers also employ consultants and may be able to refer you.

Franchises

Precision Auto Wash, 748 Miller Dr. SE, Leesburg, VA 22075, (703) 777-9095, www.precision-auto-wash.com

Helpful Government Agencies

IRS, 1111 Constitution Ave. NW, Washington, DC 20224, (800) 829-1040, (202) 622-5000, www.irs.gov

Small Business Administration, Answer Desk, P.O. Box 34500, Washington, DC 34500, (800) 827-5722, e-mail: answerdesk@sba.gov, www.sba.gov

U.S. Census Bureau, Washington, DC 20233, (301) 457-4608, www.census.gov

Insurance

Independent Insurance Agents of America, 127 S. Peyton St., Alexandria, VA 22314, (703) 683-4422, www.iiaa.org

The Insurancenter, a company that specializes in insuring car washes, 2901 Arizona Ave., Joplin, MO 64802, (800) 444-8675, www.carwashinsurance.com

National Association of Professional Insurance Agents, 400 N. Washington St., Alexandria, VA 22314, (703) 835-9340, www.pianet.com

Mailing Lists

www.listsnow.com, a Web site that provides a general idea of what types of mailing lists are available and what they cost

The Direct Marketing Association, 1120 Ave. of the Americas, New York, NY 10036-6700, (212) 768-7277, www.the-dma.org

Manufacturers and Suppliers

Dultmeier Sales, 13808 Industrial Rd., P.O. Box 45565, Omaha, NE 68145, (800) 228-9666, fax: (402) 333-5546, e-mail: dultmeier@dultmeier.com, www.dultmeier.com

Hanna-Sherman International Inc., 2000 S.E. Hanna Dr., Portland, OR 97222, (800) 288-6927, fax: (503) 659-0631, www.hanna-sherman.com

Hi-Performance Wash Systems Inc., 3901 E. 41st Ave., Denver, CO 80216, (303) 322-2232, fax: (303) 322-3307, e-mail: hpws@aol.com, www.hpws.com

PDQ Manufacturing Inc., 1698 Scheuring Rd., DePere, WI 54115, (800) 227-3373, fax: (920) 983-8330, www.pdqinc.com

Powerain Systems Inc., One Enterprise Dr., Tower, MN 55790, (800) 943-8866, fax: (218) 753-4206, e-mail: info@powerain.com, www.powerain.com

Shade Concepts, 18001 Skypark Cir., Ste. H, Irvine, CA 92614, (877) 887-4233, www.shadeconcepts.com

Publications

American Clean Car Magazine, 500 N. Dearborn St., Chicago, IL 60610, (312) 337-7700

Auto Laundry News, 2125 Center Ave., #305, Fort Lee, NJ 07024, (201) 592-7007

Professional Carwashing & Detailing Magazine, National Trade Publications, 13 Century Hill Dr., Latham, NY 12110, (518) 783-1281, www.carwash.com

Self-Service Car Wash News Magazine, P.O. Box 6341, Grand Rapids, MI 49516, e-mail: jjjsscwn@aol.com

The Carwash Appraisal Handbook, Crowe Enterprises, 600 W. 70th St., Kansas City, MO 64113, e-mail: pcrowe@juno.com

Software

WashRemote, for keeping track of inventory, Imagine Software Solutions, 1011 Stetson Cir., Corona, CA 92882, (888) 921-4204, www.coincarwash.com

Sources of Referrals

The American Bar Association, 541 N. Fairbanks Ct., Chicago, IL 60611, (312) 988-5522, www.aba.org

The American Institute of Certified Public Accountants, 1211 Ave. of the Americas, New York, NY 10036, www.aicpa.org

National Association of Insurance and Financial Advisors, 2901 Telestar Ct., P.O. Box 12012, Falls Church, VA 22042, (703) 770-8100, www.naifa.org

National Association of Small Business Accountants, 526 Davis St., #217, Evanston, IL 60201, (866) 296-0001, www.smallbizaccounts.com

The National Council of Architectural Registration Boards, 1801 K St. NW, #1100K, Washington, DC 20006-1310, (202) 783-6500, www.ncarb.org

Successful Entrepreneurs

Mike Genewick, Carson Car Wash, 225 E. Carson St., Carson, CA 90745, (310) 830-5600

Dick Hollingshead, Hollingshead Industries (Gem Autowash), 6360 Belleau Wood Lane, #1, Sacramento, CA 95822

Richard Koche, Car Love, 7225 W. 151st St., Orlando Park, IL 60462, (708) 429-3535

Web Sites

CarWashConsignment.com, a meeting place for buyers and sellers of car wash equipment, www.carwashconsignment.com

The Carwash Forum, a Web site where car wash owners gather to discuss the business, www.carwashforum.com

Glossary

"3 and 1": typical setup for a self-service wash; refers to a wash consisting of three self-service bays and one in-bay automatic unit.

Automatic rollover: see *In-bay automatic*.

Bay: the physical structure housing self-service or automatic rollover equipment.

Conveyor: a motorized track that pulls a car or truck so that washing machinery cleans the car.

Cycle: a period of time for which a self-service wash operates; usually around four minutes.

Detail: services related to cleaning the interior of an automobile.

Exterior-conveyor (or exterior-only): a type of wash that uses a conveyor system but does not include any interior cleaning.

Full-service car wash: a type of wash that includes a complete wash of the exterior, as well as cleaning of the interior of a vehicle.

ICA: International Carwash Association.

In-bay automatic (or automatic rollover): a type of wash consisting of a machine that moves, or rolls over, a stationary vehicle.

Menu of services: the list of services or wash packages a company provides.

Offline services: extra cleaning services (such as vacuuming or carpet/upholstery cleaning) performed that are not part of the standard wash process; also nonwash-related services such as oil change, quickie lube, etc.

Phase I environmental study: a study, which can limit your liability for environmental damage by calculating the amount of damage already done to a site by a previous owner.

Return on investment (ROI): a method of calculating the attractiveness of an investment; ROI is computed by dividing annual profit by the amount of money invested in the enterprise.

Run-off: water that has been used in the wash process.

Self-service car wash: a type of wash where the customer washes the car himself using equipment supplied by the car wash operator.

Stacking space: the area available on your lot where cars can wait for washing equipment to become free.

Start-up: the first cycle for a self-service wash.

Touch-free system (also called touchless): a washing system that uses high-pressure water jets, as opposed to a brush-based system, to clean a car's exterior.

Tunnel: the physical structure that houses a conveyor washing system.

Up-sell: the practice of selling additional, or more expensive, goods or services to a customer who initially wants to buy a less expensive product.

Wand: the piece of equipment self-service customers use to dispense and spread water, soap, wax, and other materials over an automobile.

Water hardness: a measure of metal salts present in water; water which is hard (more than five grains) can leave spots on cars when dry.

Weep system: a system designed to prevent freezing in pipes and wands by allowing a slow trickle of water to escape the machinery.

Index

A

Accountant, hiring a,
  40–41, 42, 119–121,
  158
Advertising, 131,
  133–134
  graph of self-service
    owners use of
    various media,
    131
  media, 133–134
  word-of-mouth, 134
Advice from successful
  car wash entrepre-
  neurs, 151–154
Amenities
  providing extra on-
    site, 36,
    114–118
  proximity to other,
    29, 137
Annual revenue, pro-
  jecting, 109–113
Appendix, 155–158

Architect, hiring a,
  42–43, 158
Attendants checklist, 90
Attorney, hiring a,
  40–41, 48, 158
Automatic dryers, 69
Automotive services,
  things to consider
  before including
  "additional,"
  117–118

B

Bottom line, boosting
  your, 36, 116–118
Business
  acumen, 149
  structure, choosing
    a, 40–41
Buying
  an existing car wash
    business, 43–44,
    69
  vs. leasing land, 44,
    45, 47

C

Capture rate, factors
  affecting, 25
Cash flow, smart,
  154
Cashiers, 90–91
Change machines,
  66–67
Changes in industry,
  adapting to, 5–7
Charity
  partnerships/dona-
  tions, 40, 112,
  139–140
Choosing a wash, fac-
  tors customers' con-
  sider when, 17
Cleaning your facility,
  34–35, 36–37
Cleanliness standards,
  16, 36–37
Community goodwill,
  generating, 40,
  139–140

▲

Competition
   differentiating yourself
      from the, 123–124,
      152
   obvious and subtle, 26–27
   proximity to your, 147
   researching your, 18–20, 21
Computer system/peripherals,
   55–57
Consolidation, industry, 5
Convenience store
   on-site, 36, 85, 116
   partnership with neighbor-
      ing, 29, 137
Conveyor car wash. *See*
   Exterior-conveyor car wash
Core business
   blurring of your, 6–7, 19
   expanding your, 144–145
Coupons, 33, 136
   book of, 134–135
   mass mailing of, 124–125,
      127
Cross-merchandising/market-
   ing, 19, 137
Customer
   access to you, 32, 33, 136
   amenities, offering multi-
      ple, 19, 36
   coffee, free, 140
   convenience, 18
   database, 128–130
   debunking myths and prej-
      udices of, 132
   demanding and time con-
      strained, 5–6, 7, 18,
      152–153
   frequent-buyer program,
      129, 136–137, 139
   lawsuits, 37, 40
   loyalty, 150–151
   professional association sta-
      tistical data on poten-
      tial, 15, 17
   relations policies, 19, 33,
      51, 140, 151

research, 16–21
service, 100–101, 147
types and traits of potential, 14–15, 129
value, providing, 18–19
"what they want," 16–19,
   133, 152–153

D

Daily routine
   of full-service and exterior-
      conveyor wash owner,
      32–33
   of self-service wash owner,
      33–36
Damage policies, 33, 52
Database marketing, 128–130
Demographic research, 27
Detailing service, 118
Direct mail campaign,
   124–127, 129–130, 134
Discounts, 29, 33, 127
   one-day only, 136
Distributors, relationship with
   your, 61–62, 149–150
Door-to-door marketing,
   127–128

E

Economic downturn, effect of
   on car wash industry, 152
Employees, 87–106
   background checks, 93
   college student, 92–93
   dedicated, 150
   developing a manual for,
      103–106
   evaluating local pool of
      potential, 29–30, 147
   incentive program, 98–99
   insurance benefits, 99
   legal complications of pay-
      ing "off the books," 95
   overcoming stigma of
      "dead-end" job, 96–97
   policy, 51
   recent immigrants, 93–94

recruiting, 92–96
retaining, 97–99, 148
retirees, 93
scheduling, 32, 35
"send-off," 33
terminating, 102–103
tips/bonuses, 97
training programs, 99–101,
   150
wages, 73, 89, 148
Environmental issues, 47–50,
   132, 153
Equipment
   checklist, 56–57
   energy efficient, 153
   exterior-conveyor and full-
      service, 68–69
   maintenance and repair of,
      32, 35, 148–149
   new vs. used, 62–63
   office, 55–60
   price vs. reliability, 63–64
   repair person, 42
   retail/lot, 69–73
   self-service, 64–67
   wash-related, 61–69
Existing car wash business,
   projecting annual revenue
   from, 109
Expansion
   equipping your car wash
      for future, 151
   into other services or prod-
      ucts, 144–145
Experts, hiring, 41–43, 158
Exterior-conveyor car wash, 2,
   9, 10, 11
   average advertising budget,
      141
   average monthly gross
      income, 115
   chart of monthly income/
      expenses for, 121
   customers, 15, 18
   daily routine of owner,
      32–33

equipment, 68–69
pricing, 84, 111–113
projected annual revenue, 111–113
start-up costs, 74–75

F

Financial management, 118–119
Financing, start-up, 73
Fleet washing, 15
Floor heater, 65
Franchises, 156
Free wash with gas fill-up, 6–7, 19, 27
Frequent-buyer program, 129, 136–137
Full-service car wash, 3, 9, 10, 11, 36
    average monthly gross income for, 115
    customers, 15, 18, 24
    daily routine, 32–33
    equipment, 68–69
    monthly income/expenses for, 120
    projected annual revenue, 111–113
    quality of service, 18
    start-up costs, chart of, 74–75
Furniture, office, 60
Future of industry, 7

G

Garbage receptacles, 71
Gas station
    competition, 6–7, 19, 27, 68
    on-site, 36, 85
    partnership with neighboring, 29
Gift shops, 116
Glossary, 159–160
Goals, defining your, 36
Government agencies, 156
Graffiti, cleaning up, 34
Grand opening, 137–139

Growth of your business, 9, 36
    long term-considerations, 143–154

H

Hands-on business, 3–4, 154
Holiday specials, 136

I

Impact fees, 28
In-bay automatic car wash (self-service), 3, 9, 10, 11, 33–36, 66, 67–68
    average gross income per bay, 115
    customers, 15
    dramatic increase of in self-service operations, 154
    monthly income/expenses for, 122
    pricing, 83–84
    projected annual revenue from, 111
    start-up costs, 76–77
Income and expenses, 107–122
Incorporating, 40–41
Industry overview, 1–11
Insurance
    agent, hiring a, 42
    coverage, list of essential, 43
    resources, 157, 158
Inventory
    and consideration of profit margins, 82
    management, 79–82
    offline car-care items, 80, 82
    offline items unrelated to car care, 80, 82
    retail items, 80, 81
    software, 81, 158

J

Job descriptions, writing, 94–95

L

Labor pool, evaluating local, 29, 147
Landscaping, 72–73
Lawsuits
    avoiding, 37
    protection from, 40
Lawyer, hiring a, 40–41, 48, 158
Leasing
    terms, 44–48
    your extra space, 118
Licensing requirements, 40, 47–48, 50
Lighting, 71–72
Limited liability company (LLC), 40–41
Local government, forming an alliance with, 27–28, 40, 147, 153
Location, 23–30
    as essential for success, 147
    assessing types of customers in chosen, 10–11, 27
    capitalizing on great, 47
    street position, 26, 147
Long-term considerations, 143–154
Lot size, 44–45, 147

M

Mailing list
    broker, 126
    for direct mail advertising, 125–127
    resources, 157
Manufacturers, list of, 157
Market research, 19–20
    checklist, 21
Marketing, 123–140
    door-to-door, 127–128
    methods, 142
Marketing plan, 123–141
    measuring the success of your, 140–141, 142

▲

Materials, car wash, 80
Mechanical skill, owner's, 148–149
Menu of services, 84–86
Mission statement, 51–52
Multiple services, 6–7, 19, 36
Myths, debunking car wash business, 3–4, 96–97, 132

N

Naming your car wash, 50–51
Neighborhood demographics, 27
New car wash
  building a, 43–44
  projecting annual revenue from, 109–113
Niche, finding a, 15–16
Non-customers
  price as prohibitive factor for, 128
  winning over, 14, 17

O

Office equipment and supplies, 55–60
  furniture, 60
  miscellaneous, 59–60
Offline services, adding, 116, 144–145
Oil change service, 118, 144
One-stop shopping, 6–7, 19, 36, 116–118
Operating costs, 113–114, 120–122
Option
  to buy, 47
  to renew lease, 45, 47
OSHA investigations, 36
Oversized car washes, 14, 15–16

P

Packages, wash, 85–86
  increasing revenue through addition of extensive, 151–152

Partnerships, 40–41
Personality traits for success in the car wash business, 7–9
  self quiz, 8
Pet washing, 116
Premium deals, 134–135
Price of lease, 46–47
Pricing, 16–19, 82–84, 109–113, 128, 147–148
  policy, 51
Product sales
  and placement, 133
  expanding, 144–145
Professional associations
  benefits of membership in, 15, 109–110
  list of, 155–156
Professional expertise, availing oneself of, 41–43
Professional manager, hiring a, 4, 101–102, 144
Profit potential of car wash business ownership, 10–11
  importance of location in determining, 10–11
Projected revenue, 109–113
Promotions, special, 134
Public relations, 137–140

Q

Quick lube, 144

R

Rainy days, 3–4, 28–29
  customer "insurance" for, 138
  rescheduling employees due to, 32, 33
Rate of return, 73, 108–109
Regulatory issues, 40, 47–48, 50, 153
Remodeling, 65–66
Repair person, equipment, 42
Repeat customers, 150–151
Resources, car wash, 155–158
Retail/lot equipment, 69–73

Return on Investment (ROI), calculating, 114
Revenue streams, additional, 114–118
Risk, evaluating, 108
Road expansion, perils of, 28
Rollover car wash (self-service), 3, 9, 10, 11
Running your business, 31–37

S

S corporation, 40–41
Safety, 36–37
Satellite locations, opening, 145
Seasonal business, 28–29
Security system, 70–71
Self-service car wash, 3, 9, 10, 11
  attendants, 87–88
  average monthly gross income per bay, 115
  coin-operated brush-and-hose combinations, 3
  customers, 14, 18, 24
  daily routine of owner, 33–36
  graph of customer wash cycles, 110
  monthly income/expenses for, 122
  pricing, 83
  projecting annual revenue from, 109–113
  start-up costs, chart of, 76–77
  wall covering, 70
Selling your business, 145–146
Service and quality, providing, 147
Service writers/greeters, 84–85, 88–90, 148
  commissions, 33
  communication system, 100
Services, menu of, 84–86

as sales tool, 85

expanding, 144–145

Setting up shop, 39–52

Shade system, 69–70

Signage

exterior, 26, 127, 130–131, 147

interior, 68, 72, 84–86, 127, 131, 133

Size of lot, 44–45

Snack shops, 116, 117

Software, 58

database marketing, 128

inventory, 158

Sole proprietorship, 40–41

Specials, "one-day only," 135–136

Spot-free rinse, 117

Start-up costs

sample of two hypothetical businesses, full-service and exterior-conveyor, 74–75

sample of two hypothetical businesses, self-service and in-bay automatic unit, 76–77

Start-up expenses, 53–77

overview of, 53–55

Success, necessary factors for, 146–150

Successful car wash entrepreneurs, 158

advice from, 151–154

Suppliers

list of, 157

reliable, 149–150

Supplies, basic, 80

T

Tales from the trenches, 151–154

Taxes, 40–41, 42, 119–121

Technicians, 91

Telephone system, 58–59

Theft

deterring, 35, 112

employee, 93

loss of revenue from, 117

Theme wash, 125

Time "squeezed" customers, 5–6, 7, 18, 152–153

Tokens, pros and cons of, 112

Trade publications, 157

Traffic

flow, researching, 24–25, 147

patterns, researching, 25, 147

Troubleshooting, daily, 32–33

Tunnels, conveyor, 68–69

Types of car washes, 2–3, 6

choosing one that "fits" you, 9–11

comparison chart, 10

investment vs. profit potential of different, 9–11, 36

U

Utility rate increases, 153

V

Vacuum services, 65, 67, 69, 111, 115–116, 127

Valuing your business for sale, 145–146

Vending machines, 67, 80, 111, 114–115, 116

W

Wash-related equipment, 61–69

Water

bills, 153

heater system, 69

permits/regulations, 47–50

reclamation systems, 64, 65, 69

shortages/droughts, 153

softening system, 48–50, 64–65, 69

Weather

effect of on business, 3–4, 28–29, 152

rescheduling employees due to, 32, 33

Web sites, car wash industry related, 158

Weep system, 65

Word-of-mouth advertising, 134

Z

Zoning regulations, 27–28, 153

Start-Up Guides
Books
Software

To order our catalog call 800-421-2300.
Or visit us online at smallbizbooks.com